WITH
THE CAMELIERS IN PALESTINE.

A. J. Astley
16 Cedar Avenue
Ellesmere
Shropshire
SY12 9PA

JUNE
2005

Representatives of I.C.C.

From left: Australian, British, New Zealand, Indian (Sikh).

WITH THE
CAMELIERS IN PALESTINE

BY

JOHN ROBERTSON

Formerly of the Fourth Battalion of the Imperial
Camel Brigade, T. Major New Zealand Mounted
Rifles, and Assistant-Director of Education to
the New Zealand Mounted Brigade in Egypt.

With Introductions by

GENERAL SIR HARRY CHAUVEL,
G.C.M.G., K.C.B.
Commander of Desert Mounted Corps

and

COLONEL THE HON. SIR JAMES ALLEN,
G.C.M.G., K.C.B., T.D.
Minister of Defence in New Zealand
during the Great War.

THIS BOOK IS A SLIGHT TRIBUTE

TO THE MEMORY OF THE

THREE HUNDRED AND FORTY-SIX MEMBERS

OF THE

IMPERIAL CAMEL BRIGADE

WHO, GATHERED FROM THE CENTRE AND THE EXTREMES
OF THE EMPIRE, GAVE THEIR LIVES TO FREE THE HOLY
LAND FROM OPPRESSION.

INTRODUCTION

BY

GENERAL SIR HARRY CHAUVEL, G.C.M.G., K.C.B.,

COMMANDER OF DESERT MOUNTED CORPS.

MAJOR ROBERTSON is doing a great service to his old comrades in publishing this History of the New Zealand Companies of the Camel Corps. In New Zealand as in Australia, it is only natural that more interest has been shown in the Western theatre of the Great War than in the Eastern theatres as the great bulk of their soldiers served in the former. The Palestine campaign is consequently little known in these countries. Nevertheless, that campaign has been more used as a " text book " for the examination of officers in the British Army than any other phase of the Great War. In fact it bids fair to take the place of Stonewall Jackson's campaign in the Shenandoah Valley which had been used for this purpose for several generations before the Great War. In spite of the fact that no American troops fought in Palestine, Lord Allenby's campaign is better known in the United States Army, particularly in the cavalry, than it is in Australia and New Zealand whose troops played such an important part in it.

Owing to its extreme mobility and suitability for desert warfare, The Imperial Camel Corps Brigade had many and varied roles to fill, all of which were filled with credit to the brigade and its gallant leader. The map of Egypt and the Sinai Peninsula is better known to its members than to any other troops. In Palestine where there is little desert, the particular value of their camels largely disappeared, but the brigade held its own with the cavalry in the fighting round Beersheba, the pursuit up the Philistine Plain, and the raid on Amman. After their transformation to cavalry, as the 14th and 15th

Australian Light Horse Regiments and the 2nd New Zealand Machine Gun Squadron, the Australian and New Zealand "Cameliers" well upheld their traditions in the Battle of Megiddo and the advance on, and capture of, Damascus.

The memory of the Imperial Camel Brigade is being perpetuated in the Australian Army by the 14th and 15th Light Horse Regiments, the motto of the latter (incidentally my own regiment) being "Nomina Desertis Inscripsimus" ("In the Desert we have written our names"), and its crest, the date-palm tree of the Desert Mounted Corps.

I have read this book with much interest and commend it to the people of New Zealand. It gives a short but graphic account of the campaign in Egypt, Palestine and Syria, and contains much interesting information about the Holy Land.

HARRY CHAUVEL,

GENERAL,

Late commanding The Desert Mounted Corps.

Melbourne.

INTRODUCTION

BY

SIR JAMES ALLEN, G.C.M.G., K.C.B., T.D.,
MINISTER OF DEFENCE IN NEW ZEALAND DURING THE
GREAT WAR.

JOHN ROBERTSON, B.A., B.SC., the author of this book, was Inspector of Schools in Otago when he volunteered for service with the New Zealand Expeditionary Force at the end of 1915. He arrived in Egypt in January, 1917, and was posted to the Imperial Camel Brigade in February.

The armistice between the Allies and Turkey came into force on the 31st October, 1918, but the New Zealanders did not leave Egypt for repatriation till July, 1919. On the 29th December, 1918, Robertson became a 2nd Lieutenant and Temporary Major, and with this rank he was appointed Assistant Director of Education to the New Zealand Expeditionary Force, which was, before its departure, located at Rafa in Egypt. In this capacity he served till the embarkation and also during the return voyage on the s.s. *Ulimaroa*. After his return he resumed his duties as Inspector of Schools, becoming Chief Inspector in Southland and later in Auckland.

The story of the Imperial Camel Brigade (or Imperial Camel Corps as it was generally known) from 1916 to 1918 has not been adequately told, and the author of this book has filled a gap in providing a very interesting record of unique experiences during the campaign in Sinai and Palestine. He was well qualified to do this as he served in the 16th Camel Company from the time of his enlistment till the brigade was disbanded in June, 1918.

Colonel Guy Powles, c.m.g., d.s.o., in his book, *The New Zealanders in Sinai and Palestine,* alludes to the formation of the Imperial Camel Corps Brigade, but makes only slight references to their activities.

Readers will be fascinated with the story of the " Camel " as told in Chapter III and with the numerous photographs descriptive of the animal which will adorn the book. No doubt they will endorse the claim made that " New Zealanders would hold themselves up as authorities on these animals and all things connected with them." That the claim is quite justified so far as the writer of the book is concerned can be realized from the description he gives of the animals, what they eat, and also because of the many references to what has been written about them, starting with the story in the Book of Genesis—of the camel forming part of a shady transaction that Abraham had with Pharaoh regarding Sarai, his wife, and leading up to Kinglake's description in *Eothan* of the crossing of the Sinai desert about the year 1860.

In this same Chapter III it is claimed that " to be of some practical value a treatise on the camel needs to give a detailed analysis of the physical, mental, and moral qualities (if it has any of the latter)." The reader will find evidence of mental activities, which are of a type not unknown to the human being, but possibly more vigorous. The moral qualities are probably not lacking, but as with the ordinary man, the evidence of them is often not very clear.

Chapter II tells of the growth of the I.C.C. to a brigade of two thousand eight hundred, of which the two New Zealand companies provided twelve officers and three hundred and thirty-eight other ranks.

As the campaign progressed we learn that the camel country was passed over; the brigade was reorganized into a cavalry force and " the Australian and New

Zealand Cameliers said good-bye to their camels, which had carried them in comfort over desert and wilderness." The training for campaigning, the nature of the country in the Sinai desert and elsewhere, with the difficulties appertaining to lack of water supply, are graphically described.

As to the part taken by the I.C.C. the reader is told of the fights on the border line between Sinai and Palestine in Chapter VIII, of the failure of the first two attacks on Gaza (Chapters IX and X), and how Beersheba and Gaza were captured, in Chapter XIV. In this same chapter is a very interesting record of the Gaza to Beersheba line, through the centre of which the Camel Corps and other troops carried on a pursuit of the retreating Turks for some seventy-five miles.

General Allenby took over the command in June, 1917, and six months later Jerusalem was surrendered "without a shot being fired in its immediate vicinity."

In Chapter XXI we read of the "Big break through" when "The Cavalry Force advanced fifty miles in twenty-four hours, made a raid on Nazareth to attempt to capture the Turkish Commander-in-Chief, Marshal Liman von Sanders, and his Staff. It is said Liman von Sanders hurriedly departed in a motor car clad only in his night attire."

The author's knowledge of history has enabled him to enlighten the story of the fighting and educate the reader by very many historical references, dating from the passage of forces across the Sinai Peninsula, 4000 B.C., down to 1191 A.D. when Richard the Lion Heart with 100,000 Crusaders defeated 300,000 Saracens under their renowned leader Saladin.

The story is also brightened by references to the daily life of the men, and much interest will attach to the reading of chapters which tell of "The Visit to the

Dentist," " All in the Day's Work," and Chapter XX,
" Cameliers at Play."

This foreword must not end without calling attention to the very interesting reference in Chapter XXII to
the Plain of Esdraelon, about which Mr. Robertson
writes: " No other level space of ground of equal size
on the surface of the earth could muster such a gathering of the harvest of war. Is it to be wondered at that
the writer of the Book of Revelation should select this
plain as the site of the Battle of Armageddon, the final
battle between the forces of good and evil? It is from
Megiddo, the supposed site of Armageddon, that Lord
Allenby has taken his title, Viscount Allenby of
Megiddo." In reading this same chapter one's feelings
are soothed and at the same time stimulated by the
reminder that, near that same plain within sight of
Nazareth, " in a humble carpenter's house was reared
the Son of Man."

J. ALLEN.

Dunedin.

Preface

THE granting to the British of the mandate over Palestine after the Great War has made this historic country of greater interest than ever to the British public. The recent dissensions between the Arabs and the Jews, both races with traditional claims to its possession, have brought it more prominently into public notice, while the official opening in January, 1935, of the immense pipe lines carrying oil from Kirkuk, one hundred and fifty miles north of Bagdad in Irak, across the barren desert of Arabia, the high plateau of Transjordania, the deep valley of the Jordan, Northern Palestine and Syria, to the ports of Haifa and Tripoli on the Mediterranean Sea, has given to Britain an important commercial interest in this ancient land.

How this interesting country was wrested from the hands of the Turks by the British Army under Lord Allenby, has been described both officially and unofficially, but the story of one unusual unit of this force, The Imperial Camel Corps, is still unknown to the general public.

Never before in modern times had such a large organized force of troopers been mounted on camels— the animals specially adapted by nature for transport in the desert—and, owing to the advancement that has been made in mechanical methods of warfare, both on land and in the air, it is not likely that such a force will ever again be used on such a scale.

In this book an attempt has been made to include an account of the everyday experiences of the Cameliers, as well as to link up their achievements with the major military operations, while the historical aspect of the country has also been touched on.

13

It may be objected that this makes a disjointed narrative, but if this is so, the whole campaign was disjointed; while major operations were being planned or carried out, the men in the ranks were having their daily experiences, monotonous, humorous, or tragic, in the midst of scenes of greater historic interest than can be found in any other country in the world. This latter interest appealed to all ranks. I have seen a group of a dozen men lying round a trooper who had a copy of the Bible, and who was reading out the story of Samson at Gaza, and wherever the column moved, inquiries were constantly made as to the history attached to the places passed. But frequently military exigencies overshadowed historic interest—we were making history.

After the reorganization of the Australian and New Zealand Companies of the I.C.C. into the 5th Australian Light Horse Brigade, with its attached New Zealand Machine Gun Squadron (No. 2), these ex-Cameliers took an active part in Lord Allenby's great sweep north through Samaria and Syria. This story has not been fully related in this country, and an account of it has been included in this volume.

It is not claimed that anything like justice has been done to the deeds of the various Companies of the Camel Brigade, but it has been impossible to obtain access to the official diaries of overseas companies. As the doings of his own Company, the Sixteenth, are better known to the writer than those of other units, these bulk more largely than those of any of the others. This must not be taken as an indication that this company took a more prominent part in the campaign than did these others, but the work of one may be taken as typical of the work done by all. Each company did its share, and did it well, and this book is a slight attempt to bring before the public the efforts of a gallant body of men who bore their part in the struggle against a no mean foe.

The movements of the various forces as here described are strictly in accordance with official accounts, such as the Despatches of General Murray and General Allenby, and *Military Operations, the Official History of the War,* published by H.M. Stationery Office, 1930.

I have to thank several old comrades for assistance, both as regards furnishing material for subject matter, and also for illustrations.

To General Sir H. Chauvel, formerly Commander of the Anzac Mounted Division, and later of Desert Mounted Corps, who commanded the whole of the Cavalry Force in Palestine and Syria during General Allenby's command, and who supplied the driving power during the final cavalry sweep north through Samaria, Galilee, and Syria, and to Sir James Allen, who was Minister of Defence in New Zealand during the whole of the Great War, I tender my sincere thanks for their kind introductory notes.

J. R.

47 Highgate, Roslyn,
  Dunedin, New Zealand.

Contents

LIST OF ILLUSTRATIONS

LIST OF ILLUSTRATIONS

MAPS

CHAPTER I

ON OUTPOST IN THE WADI EL ARISH

The evening meal is over in the camp of the Sixteenth N.Z. Company of the Fourth Battalion of the I.C.C., which is situated some fifteen miles from the mouth of the Wadi El Arish, on the eastern border of the Sinai Peninsula—this Wadi is marked on all Biblical maps of this country as the River of Egypt, which appears a misnomer, as it is at least a hundred miles from what is popularly looked on as the eastern border of Egypt— the Suez Canal, and water is very seldom seen in it.

The sun has set, and the shadows of evening are falling along the dry bed of the Wadi and on the low undulating country on each side of it, giving a softer appearance to the scattered stunted scrub which, in the bright light of the April sun, stands out sharply from the white sand on which it grows, the short dark shadows of the scrub, interspersed with the sunlit spaces between, giving a draught-board appearance to the landscape which is toned down as the shadows lengthen.

Four men have orders to report to the orderly tent for outpost duty. They are instructed by the sergeant-major to proceed up the Wadi for eight miles along the old track used by the Arabs and their predecessors for countless generations, and there take up a position so as to command all approaches towards the camp from the south. They are once more impressed with the instructions, which have already appeared in routine orders, that all mounted bodies approaching from the interior of the country in the direction of the camp are to be looked on as enemies. Reports have been received by the O.C. that a large force of Turkish cavalry, said to be two thousand strong, is concentrating in the low hilly country to the south-east, for the purpose of

21

working in behind the British army and cutting its lines of communication with its base on the canal.

The four Cameliers equip themselves for their night duty, and, in spite of the protesting groans of the "hoostas," mount and ride off into the deepening twilight, with the facetious remarks in their ears from the sentry as to the possibilities of their landing in Constantinople before long, or of being employed as batmen to a Turkish corporal in the near future.

Three miles out another outpost is passed, and the four ride on, with the peculiar swinging strides of the camels making little sound in the silence of the desert. The leader selects a suitable spot where a small wadi enters at right angles to the main one, a line of low cliffs on its farther side preventing any approach from that direction, while away on the right across the main wadi, stretch miles and miles of low undulating sand-hills, all well under observation from the post selected. The Wadi is from a quarter to half a mile wide, its surface consisting partly of gravel, and partly of dry clay and sand washed down in the rainy seasons, but now as dry as—well, nothing can be drier than the Wadi El Arish in the month of April.

The camels are "barracked" in a low hollow, and the men draw lots for the order of duties. This done, number one takes up his post in a commanding position, while the other three wrap themselves in their overcoats, with their loaded rifles beside them, and on the dry ground soon drop off to sleep. At the end of two hours the sentry on duty wakes up number two, then settles down for the remainder of the night—as he hopes. It is a still, cloudy night, with sufficient broken clouds to obscure the light of the stars. Number two stands leaning against the low bank of the tributary wadi, his gaze bent along the track in the darkness, while his thoughts try to figure out his relationship to the rest of the military world of which he is only a unit. He is, as it were, a nerve point thrust out to feel the slightest touch to the parent body, his duty is to transmit this knowledge instantly and accurately along the nerve or line of communication to the supporting outpost, which in turn passes it back to the company, to be transmitted by the latter to the battalion, thence to the brigade, which then forwards it to Divisional Headquarters, and so to Corps Commander, and finally to the General Officer commanding the whole army. What a responsibility, he moralises, rests on the nerve point! If it fails to receive the impression or fails to transmit it along the nerve line, why, the two thousand Turkish cavalry will sweep down on the sleeping company, then possibly wipe out the battalion, the whole brigade will be endangered, the army may have to fall back, and the whole military position, so laboriously built up, will fall like a set of dominoes standing on end.

On April 23, 1916, at Katia and Oghratina in the Sinai Peninsula, the nerve point had not functioned properly, with the result that three squadrons of Yeomanry were wiped out, and the Anzac Division had to be hurried across the canal to save the situation, as the safety of the canal was imperilled.

And so the lonely sentry in the Wadi becomes impressed with the importance of his position. Hush! What was that sound? Only a night bird out in the waste on the right. Its cry reminds him of the cry of the weka in his native New Zealand—but there are no wekas in the Sinai desert. Might it not be the signal of an enemy? He listens intently, but there is no reply to the call. But what was that? Something like the murmur of a human voice away in the distance ahead, and surely that was the sound of a hoof striking a stone, and then another voice-like sound. He stirs up his mates, directing one to go down into the bed of the main Wadi, where he will have a clear getaway if necessary to warn the next outpost; the other two are placed where they will best cover the ground in front and on flank, while the leader takes a position where the age-old track crosses the bed of the side wadi. Sure enough muffled voices ahead are heard, and then the steps of animals. Nothing can be seen as yet, but on they come. Are they the advanced guard of a larger force? The leader waits till the party is within hail. " Istanna, andak, aulad! "[1] he calls, opening and closing the breach of his rifle to let them know that he is armed and ready. A reply comes back in a quavering voice in a foreign tongue, which certainly does not give the impression of a military owner. " Ta'ala hene, ista'gil! "[2] he orders. (He has been in the country only two months, and is already proud of his knowledge (?) of Arabic.) Again a tremulous voice replies, and now he thunders out, " Ta'ala hene, higgury! higgury! "[3] while he covers with his rifle the spot where the intruders appear to be. Presently a dark shape looms forward in the darkness, then another, and two camels, loaded with bundles of stunted stalks of barley, and led by two trembling Bedouins, approach, and the latter immediately begin to palaver in their own tongue, but the sight of a fixed bayonet on a loaded rifle pointed at them, reduces them to silence. They are escorted to a hollow spot, their camels are " barracked," the loads and the Bedouins themselves carefully examined to see that nothing contraband is concealed upon them, and the two mumbling wretches are made to crouch on the ground beside their animals for the remainder of the night under the watchful eye of a New Zealander, who, deprived of his night's sleep, expresses his opinion New Zealandly on all Bedouins of doubtful parentage, who wander about at

[1] " Wait, halt, boys! "
[2] and [3] " Come here! hurry! "

24

Machine-gun Company

Camel Company Advancing

Sikh Tug-of-War Team

Camel Cacolet for carrying wounded

night to harvest their barley crops (by pulling up the short straws by the roots), and pack it home on camels, some twenty miles away, to thresh it with a stick in safety and at their leisure.

The "nerve point" has functioned accurately, but decides that the "impression" is not of sufficient importance to trouble a "nerve line" to transmit it to the "brain," and so the slumbers of the G.O.C. at Headquarters are not disturbed. The visions of the two thousand Turkish cavalry vanish into thin air as the rays of the sun peep over the eastern horizon, showing nothing but a lonely featureless landscape, and the members of the outpost wend their way back to camp with their night's captures.

CHAPTER II

THE IMPERIAL CAMEL CORPS

THE Imperial Camel Corps was a cosmopolitan body of troops that gradually grew into a brigade some two thousand eight hundred strong. Companies each of six officers and one hundred and sixty-nine other ranks were formed at various times, four companies forming a battalion. By December 19, 1916, four battalions were in existence, which were combined into one organized brigade, with the necessary units, such as a machine-gun squadron, artillery, field troop, signal section, field ambulance, and detachment of the army service corps, and a brigade ammunition column.

The Brigade was composed of the First and Third Battalions, recruited from the Australian Light Horse, the Fourth Battalion, composed of two companies drawn from the Australian Light Horse, and two, the 15th and 16th Companies, from the New Zealand Mounted Rifles, and the Second Battalion which was recruited from British Yeomanry Regiments. There were two additional detached British companies. A machine-gun squadron, the 26th, was formed from drafts from the machine-gun sections of the Scottish Horse, the Lanarkshire Yeomanry and the Ayrshire Yeomanry. A mountain battery of the Hong Kong and Singapore R.G.A., composed of big brawny Sikhs, two hundred and forty strong, with six nine-pounder guns, carried on the backs of camels, formed part of the Brigade. In addition to the Machine-gun Squadron, armed with Vickers machine-guns, each company had a section (equivalent to a mounted rifle troop) equipped with three Lewis guns. The whole force was nearly equal in strength to two mounted brigades.

The field ambulance, instead of using wheeled vehicles, transported the sick and wounded in " cacolets," on the backs of camels. These consisted of two canvas stretchers balanced horizontally, one on each side of a specially constructed saddle. In these the wounded men could either sit or lie at full length, and were shaded from the sun by a small canvas hood. The jolting motion of the camel frequently was most trying to the badly wounded men, but it was sometimes a case of this kind of carriage, or death, and these camel cacolets, going as they did where wheeled transport was impossible, undoubtedly were the means of saving the lives of many wounded men who otherwise would have had a poor chance of being carried back to safety. This was especially the case when the mounted troops were fighting their way across the sands of the Sinai Peninsula during the latter half of 1916, and again, in March, 1918, when Shea's Force ploughed its way up the muddy goat-tracks on the rocky mountain-sides east of the Dead Sea, leading to Amman, where neither horse artillery nor wheeled transport could follow the advance.

The whole of the Camel Corps was mounted on camels, of which well over three thousand were required to mount the men, and carry the transport. These animals, if following each other head to tail, would make a column over eight miles long. No wheeled vehicles of any sort were attached to the Corps. As each man always had to have in stock five days' supply of food and water for himself, and a similar supply of grain for his mount, as well as over two hundred rounds of ammunition, the whole Brigade could, at an hour's notice, go off into the "blue" for five days without any communication with or assistance from its base.

During the whole of its existence the Brigade was under the command of Brigadier C. L. Smith, v.c., m.c., d.c.l.i., who had seen active service in the South African

War, and in Somaliland, and who for several years served in the Egyptian Army and in the Soudan. He served in the European War from 1914, and was employed with the Egyptian Army in 1915 in command of the Camel Corps. In December, 1916, he was appointed to the command of the newly constituted Imperial Camel Brigade, with the rank of Temporary Brigadier-General, which position he retained until the disbandment of the Brigade in June, 1918. The following extract from the *London Gazette* of June 7, 1904, relates the circumstance under which he won the Victoria Cross in the Somali War. " At the commencement of the fight at Jidballi on January 10, 1904, the enemy made a sudden and determined rush on the 5th Somali Mounted Infantry from under cover of bushes close at hand. They were supported by rifle fire, advanced very rapidly, and got right amongst our men. Lieut. Smith, Somali Mounted Infantry, and Lieut. J. R. Welland, M.D., Royal Army Medical Corps, went out to the aid of Hospital Assistant Rohamat Ali, who was wounded, and endeavoured to bring him out of action on a horse, but the rapidity of the enemy's advance rendered this impossible, and the hospital assistant was killed. Lieut. Smith then did all that any man could do to bring out Dr. Welland, helping him to mount a horse, and when that was shot, a mule. This also was hit, and Dr. Welland was speared by the enemy. Lieut. Smith stood by Dr. Welland, and when that officer was killed, was within a few paces of him, endeavouring to keep off the enemy with a revolver. At that time the Dervishes appeared to be all round him, and it was marvellous that he escaped with his life."

When Brigadier-General Smith was appointed to the command of the Imperial Camel Corps he was only thirty-eight years old, and at the time, must have been one of the youngest brigadiers in the British Army.

Mounted drill in the Brigade began with "barracking" the camels, that is causing them to adopt a kneeling position. This was brought about by the rider tugging the halter rope downwards, while at the same time he kept uttering a guttural sound, "duh, duh, duh," at every tug; he frequently made other remarks not very complimentary to the animal's parents. The camel seemed to kneel by numbers. One! Bend the lower portions of the forelegs. Two! Sink down on the lower sections of the hind legs. Three! Fold the upper portion of the front legs on top of the lower. Four! Bring down the upper parts of the hind legs above the lower. Five! Shuffle and tuck in the feet comfortably. Six! Groan.

On the order "Get ready to mount," the rider pulled round the head of the camel until it looked to the rear; he then placed his left foot on the bend of the animal's neck, and grasped with his right hand the stout peg at the back of the saddle. On the word "Mount," he raised himself briskly into the saddle, throwing his right leg over the front peg of the saddle. He then released the halter to its full length, and the camel instinctively rose to its feet. If the rider was not alert and the camel moved first, the former was liable to be thrown over the saddle. While the mounting movement was in progress, most of the camels roared like wild beasts. When the Brigade in "Column of route" was mounting, the order moved from front to rear, and those in the rear ranks could hear the movement coming towards them like the approach of breakers on an angry rock-bound seashore. When the animals rose to their feet the noise immediately stopped. On a dark night in a wadi the effect was weird. The camel has been called the "Ship of the desert," but the Camel Brigade when mounting could by no means claim to be the "Silent Service."

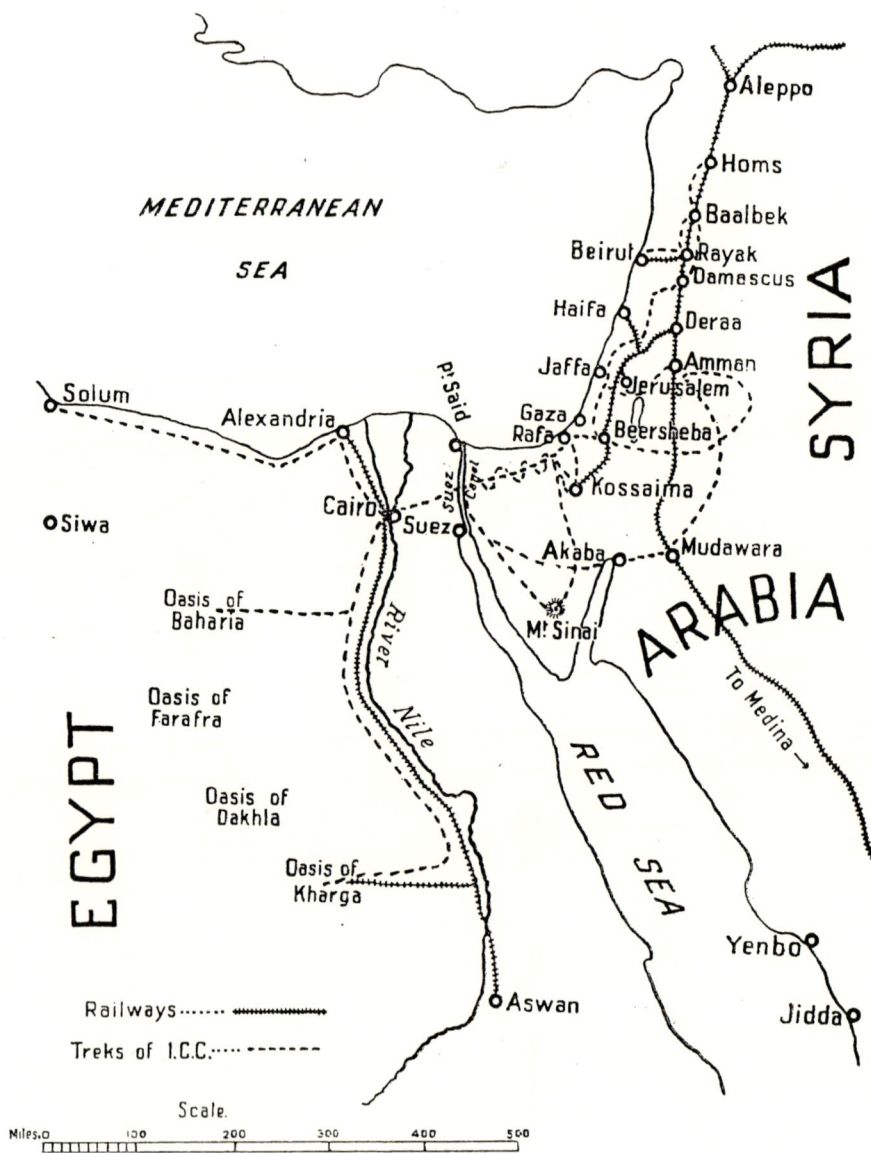

MEDITERRANEAN
SEA

SYRIA

EGYPT

ARABIA

RED SEA

Aleppo
Homs
Baalbek
Beirut
Rayak
Damascus
Haifa
Deraa
Jaffa
Amman
Jerusalem
Gaza
Rafa
Beersheba
Kossaima
Akaba
Mudawara
Mt Sinai
To Medina →
Solum
Alexandria
Pt Said
Cairo
Suez
Siwa
Oasis of
Baharia
Oasis of
Farafra
Oasis of
Dakhla
Oasis of
Kharga
River Nile
Suez Canal
Yenbo
Jidda
Aswan

Railways ·······
Treks of I.C.C. ·········

Scale.

Miles.0   100   200   300   400   500

30

The company formations were a mixture of the Infantry and Mounted Rifle systems. The unit was the "group" of four men; eight groups formed a section; four sections with Lewis gun and signal sections made up a company; four companies formed a battalion; and four battalions made up the brigade.

Each battalion had a distinguishing colour; the men of the First Battalion (Australian) under the command of Lieut.-Col. G. F. Langley, wore on their hats a red, triangular "flash" or pyramid, to give it a name more in keeping with its Oriental environment; those of the Second Battalion (British Yeomanry) under Lieut.-Col. R. Buxton, wore green flashes; the Third Battalion (Australian) under Lieut.-Col. N. B. De Lancey Forth, wore black and white; and the Fourth Battalion (Australian and New Zealand) under Lieut.-Col. A. J. Mills, wore blue.

The Headquarters Administrative Centre of the Brigade was at Abbassia on the outskirts of Cairo, not far from Heliopolis. A small but competent staff under Captain Barber, initiated the newcomers into the mysteries surrounding the camel, and soon the Colonials were handling their new chargers like natives of the country.

A Camel Remount Depot and a Camel Hospital were also established in Egypt. Camels have diseases peculiar to themselves, mange being very common amongst the animals that were procured locally. This disease, if unchecked, will destroy a camel force in the field in from three to six months. During the late War a special branch of the Veterinary Corps was trained in the treatment of camels, and so well did this department function, that an average of forty thousand camels, riding and transport, was maintained in the field during the war, seventy per cent. of the animals sent to the camel hospitals being returned to the Remount Department as fit for further service. 31

During the British advance in November and December of 1917, the camels of the Brigade had a rough time. The Cameliers were linked up with the front line for five weeks on end, and during that time advanced about one hundred miles. Sometimes the animals had only one feed a day, and for days at a time their loaded saddles were not removed from their backs. As a consequence the camels became worn out, and badly infected with mange. The force was withdrawn to Rafa, a sandy area in the south where the animals were all put under treatment by the Veterinary Service. In nine weeks men and camels were once more ready for action, and in March moved north once more, to take part in the most strenuous experience that the Brigade ever went through—the advance over the Jordan River, and the ascent of the muddy goat-tracks on the slopes of the Mountains of Moab, east of the Dead Sea.

In one of General Skobeleff's Russian campaigns in Central Asia, his force returned after some months with only one camel surviving out of a transport force of twelve thousand such animals.

In the British Afghan campaign of 1879-80 seventy thousand transport animals were lost, most of them being camels.

The Imperial Camel Brigade has the distinction of being represented by various detachments in more areas of the Middle East than any other body of troops taking part in the Eastern campaign. Some companies took part in the operations against the Senussi in the Western Desert of Egypt at the end of 1915, and beginning of 1916. It was during this campaign that Siwa was captured—a town situated in an oasis two hundred miles south from Sollum on the Mediterranean coast, near the border line between Egypt and Tripoli. Siwa, like an isolated island in an ocean of desert sand, was a ten days' march over a waterless and quite uninhabited

Ready to march

Marching Order

Vet. Sergeant at work

Watering from Well, Lahfan

waste. Its history goes back some fifteen hundred years before the beginning of the Christian era; it was the seat of a famous oracle which was held in such great veneration by the Greeks that it was visited by Alexander the Great in the year 331 B.C. in order to get a pronouncement that he was of divine origin. In the late war the oasis was captured by an armoured car raid in 1916. Shortly afterwards a force of armoured cars, under the Duke of Westminster, made a brilliant rescue of ninety-one sailors from the torpedoed vessels, the *Tara* and *Moorina,* who had been handed over by the Germans as prisoners to the Senussi. The force dashed across one hundred and twenty miles of barren desert, attacked an unknown force of the enemy, rescued the prisoners, and returned to its base in safety without a casualty.

During a part of 1916 and 1917, an Australian detachment of the I.C.C. patrolled the Oases of Baharia, Dakhla, and Kharga, which are situated west of the River Nile, and some two hundred, and three hundred and seventy miles from its mouth. They are a part of the Great Sahara Desert that extends across the whole of Africa to the shores of the Atlantic Ocean. It was across this country that Cambyses, the Persian conqueror of Egypt, in 525 B.C. sent an army of fifty thousand men to try to capture Siwa. The whole force disappeared into the desert waste, and from that day to this no trace of it has ever been discovered. The desert as well as the ocean can keep its secrets. The Persians were either overwhelmed by a violent sandstorm, or lost their way and died of hunger and thirst in the desert.

Some of the Australians came up to the I.C.C. Detail Camp at Abbassia in March, 1917, after having been on desert patrols for some months, during which time they had very few opportunities of drawing or spending their pay. Their clothes and equipment were faded and worn

33

out; they were dying with thirst, and the joys of Cairo awaited them. The camp wet canteen ran dry in an hour or two, and then they adjourned to the city. A double guard had to be put on the guardroom that night in the camp, and the accommodation was taxed to its utmost before morning. In a short time the camp authorities decided it would be best for all concerned if these troops once more adjourned to the silent wastes, and the Cameliers moved off into the unknown.

Another detachment of the I.C.C., consisting of fifty Australians with two machine-guns, made an interesting reconnaissance to Jebel Musa (Mount Sinai) in the south of the Sinai Peninsula, while in July, 1918, two British companies, three hundred strong under Colonel Buxton, marched across the Sinai Peninsula to Akaba on the eastern branch of the end of the Red Sea. There they joined up with Colonel Lawrence and his Arab forces, and trekked north parallel with the Hedjaz railway to the neighbourhood of Amman, and from there made their way back to Beersheba in the south of Palestine.

In addition to all these expeditions, various units of the I.C.C. patrolled the whole of the northern portion of the Sinai Peninsula during 1917, the Brigade took an active part in Allenby's advance through Palestine, and in the raid across the Jordan to Amman, and the Australians and New Zealanders, as members of the Fifth Light Horse Brigade, later on in 1918 took part in the great cavalry sweep north to Damascus and beyond, almost to Aleppo.

CHAPTER III

THE CAMEL

THE word " Camel " immediately brings to the minds of most people a picture of sand and Arabs, date-palms, and goat-hair tents, and a feeling of romance always associated with travel in the desert.

Before the Great War young New Zealanders had no more knowledge about camels than what they had gathered from tales of adventure, or from the sight of an occasional one in a travelling circus, and they little dreamt that before the war was ended they would hold themselves up as authorities on these animals, and all things connected with them.

A scientist says gravely that " a camel is a large tylopodous ruminant of the genus Camelus, having a humped back. There are two species, the Arabian or one-humped (*Camelus dromedarius*), and the Bactrian, or two-humped (*Camelus bactrianus*)." But this scientific description of a camel was of no use whatever to the colonial troopers when they came to handle the animals. To be of some practical value a treatise on the camel needs to give a detailed analysis of its physical, mental, and moral qualities (if it has any of the two latter).

The Arabs say that at the Creation, when the beasts of the earth were formed, there were left over a lot of remnants out of which was made a camel, and the parts are not hard to identify. The head of a sheep was placed on the neck of a giraffe, which was attached to the body of a cow, and the neck bent itself in shame at being put to such a use. The tail of an ass was appended, and the whole was set on the legs of a horse, which ended in the pads of a dog, on each of which was stuck the claw of an ostrich, and the monstrosity, evidently

35

being considered a failure, was banished to live in the desert where no other quadruped could exist, and where its solitary existence gave it " the hump." The Arabs say that the camel alone of all living things, knows what is the hundredth name of Allah, hence the supercilious expression it puts on its face when it condescends to look on a mere man. Is it to be wondered at that the camel, brooding over its hard fate, should have developed a grudge against all other created things? Thus we find that the animal has no feelings of gratitude for any kindness done to it, and has no feeling of companionship for man or beast. It will accept food from the hand, but will just as likely try to eat the hand that feeds it.

The camel has been hardly dealt with in literature. When it is first mentioned in the Bible, in the Book of Genesis, the camel is said to have formed part of a somewhat shady transaction that Abraham had with Pharaoh regarding Sarai, his wife, and later on it is said to have been afflicted by one of the plagues of Egypt, when a grievous murrain fell on the horses, asses, camels, oxen and sheep of the Egyptians, and the camel does not seem, after more than three thousand years, to have quite recovered from the affliction.

In his *New Pilgrim's Progress*, Mark Twain says: " When a camel is down on all his knees, flat on his breast to receive his load, he looks something like a goose swimming, and when he is upright he looks like an ostrich with an extra set of legs. Camels have immense, flat, forked cushions of feet, that make a track in the dust like a pie with a slice cut out of it. They are not particular about their diet. They would eat a tombstone if they could bite it. A thistle grows about here which has needles on it that would pierce through leather, I think; if one touches you, you can find relief in nothing but profanity. The camels eat these. They show by their actions that they enjoy them. I suppose

36

it would be a real treat to a camel to have a keg of nails for supper."

Kipling says of it:

"The 'orse he knows above a bit, the bullock's but a fool,
The elephant's a gentleman, the battery mule's a mule,
But the commissariat cam-u-el, when all is said and done,
'E's a devil, and a' ostrich, and a' orphan child in one."

A later writer, W. W. Gibson, says of them:

"An' then consider camels; only think
Of camels long enough, and you'ld go mad—
With all their humps and lumps, their knobbly knees,
Splay feet, and straddle legs, their sagging necks,
Flat flanks, and scraggy tails, and monstrous teeth."

Even in proverb the camel is maligned: "It is the last straw that breaks the camel's back," is often quoted. It is a physical impossibility to break a camel's back. No other quadruped has such a strong one, and if the loads that are imposed on camels were placed on horses' backs they would immediately collapse.

So it was with prejudiced minds that the New Zealanders and Australian Light Horsemen came to the camels, but after some two years' intimate experience of them in their native habitat, the men's views were considerably modified. Trooper Bluegum, in *The Cameliers,* admits this when he addresses his camel thus:

"In the days when I was younger, when I never knew your worth,
When I thought a prancing palfrey was the finest thing on earth,
When a ride upon a camel seemed a punishment for sin,
And made a man feel fed up with the land we're living in,
It was then my errant fancy lightly turned to thoughts of verse,
And I libelled you, old Hoosta, in a wild Iambic curse.
I know you now for better, but for you I might be dead,
So I recant, old Hoosta, I take back all I said.

"When winter nights were freezing on the hills of old Judaea,
You humped my load of blankets and a ton of surplus gear;
When summer's sun was scorching and my head seemed like
   to burst,
You bore a full fantassi, and quenched my raging thirst.
I have never yet gone hungry, I have never yet gone dry;
That's something to your credit in a place like Sinai.
You have been my board and lodging, you even humped my
   bed—
Honest Injun! Oont, I'm grateful; I take back all I said."

37

Owing to the peculiar cellular formation of its stomach a camel is able to retain sufficient water in it and to draw on its store at will so as to make it satisfy its requirements for four or five days. Even when camped beside a water supply the animals were watered only every third or fourth day. On one occasion, at Sheikh Nuran, a pack camel, through oversight, was missed on the regular watering day, and went for eight days without a drink—and lived. It was a sight to watch camels drinking. The saddle girths had first to be let out for two or three feet, before the animals approached the watering troughs, or the straps would have burst. The animal's body visibly swelled in all directions until it resembled a teapot on a stand, with the neck for a spout, the tail for a handle, and the hump for a lid. What sighs of contentment were uttered and how they lingered over their drinks as if in utter enjoyment, as the water trickled slowly along the whole lengths of their throats. The camel is a true toper, and was the envy of many a thirsty Camelier. When it had the opportunity to indulge, it "made it a welter." No wonder Trooper Bluegum apostrophized his mount:

> "You thirst a week unblinking,
> And when I see you drinking,
> You always set me thinking:
> Lord, I wish I had your neck."

Horses in the Eastern campaign had to be watered daily, if possible. The longest time that the horses of the New Zealand Mounted Brigade went without water was for seventy-two hours, but this was most exceptional, and was not in the hottest season, being in the month of November in 1917. It will thus be seen that in its own country the camel has a decided advantage over the horse, especially in the desert where supplies of water are few and far between.

Kinglake, in *Eothan*, in the description of his crossing the Sinai Desert about the year 1860, says: " The camel, like the elephant, is one of the old-fashioned sort of animals that still walk along the (now nearly exploded) plan of the ancient animals that lived before the Flood. It moves forward both its near legs at the same time, and then awkwardly swings round its off shoulder and haunch, so as to repeat the manoeuvre on that side; its pace therefore is an odd, disjointed, and disjoining sort of movement that is rather disagreeable at first, but you soon grow reconciled to it. The height to which you are raised is of great advantage to you in passing the burning sands of the desert, for the air at such a distance from the ground is much cooler and more lively than that which circulates beneath."

The foot of a camel is composed of two soft, broad pads somewhat like those on the foot of a dog, and these spread out when the animal is walking, and prevent it from sinking in the soft sand. The ordinary walking pace of the animal is about three miles an hour; at a jolting trot it can travel at the rate of five or six miles an hour, but if urged it can move at a much more rapid speed. I have seen a horseman trying to round up a runaway camel in the sand, but the horse, when pushed to its utmost speed, was quite unable to compete with the runaway. The utmost speed of a camel was a most uncomfortable one for its rider, but this was seldom called for on active service, except when necessity demanded. If it had been, many of the Camelier's personal possessions and " household " utensils would have strewn the desert sands.

For food for the camel each Camelier had issued to him fifty pounds of durra, a kind of millet, which was supposed to serve the animal as food for five days. When the unit was in reserve a supply of tibbin was usually issued in addition, to be mixed with the durra. Tibbin might be described as broken straw, it was too coarse to be called chaff. The camel, however, could add to his rations by cropping the stunted scrub and scattered herbage occasionally found in the wilderness.

For his own use each trooper was supplied with a fantassi containing five gallons of water. The fantassi was a zinc vessel, oval in cross-section and about thirty inches long. This supply of water was supposed to serve him for all purposes for five days. In addition he was supposed to keep five days' supply of rations (in the form of bully-beef or Machonachy rations, and army biscuits) in his saddle-bags.

The riding-saddle had a stout wooden peg at front and rear, and from these were hung horizontally the bag of durra on one side, and the fantassi of water on the other. Across the saddle were hung the two stout canvas saddle-bags containing the rider's rations, and his spare clothing and personal equipment. Above these were spread his blankets, usually four in number (two issued, the other two commandeered) neatly folded to make a comfortable seat in the hollow of the saddle. A rubber ground-sheet covered these and kept off the rain, and above all his worldly goods sat the rider, cross-legged, with his calves and feet resting on a leather apron hung from the front of the saddle over the camel's shoulders.

In addition to the above each man had always to have two hundred and fifty rounds of ammunition in his possession, a billy or can of some sort usually hung somewhere on the premises, bivvy-poles and a stock of firewood was attached wherever possible, and with water-bottle, rifle and rider, the whole load made up a total weight of about three hundred and twenty pounds, but with luxuries added it often amounted to more than three hundredweight. If the animal could not rise with this load on his back, it was understood he was too heavily loaded. If he did manage to get on his feet, he would travel with it all day, or all night, as our treks

Camelier's Equipment

Camels Feeding

Bikanir Camel

Egyptian Camel

usually took place at night, for very obvious reasons in the war zone.

On one occasion when we were training to go on a longer and more arduous stunt than usual, we were ordered to cut down our loads as severely as possible. "You know, boys," said Colonel Mills, "you can't take your drawing-room furniture with you this time."

The night before the 16th Company (New Zealanders) crossed over to the Sinai side of the Suez Canal at Ferdan, supplies of fodder had to be carted over the canal by means of pack-camels which had to balance themselves and their bulky loads on a swaying pontoon bridge whilst crossing. When the last camel of the party was loaded up with sacks of grain there was still a quantity left, but sooner than make another trip over in the gathering darkness, the packmen decided to try out the theory of "the last straw." The remaining sacks were securely lashed on top of the load of a sturdy pack-camel, and with the assistance of four men the valiant animal succeeded in getting into a standing position. There was a slight slope down to the bridge, and then the bridge itself had to be negotiated. Having no four-wheel brakes, the camel took the grade at a run on to the bridge, which swayed and groaned ominously. The pontoons dipped as the procession progressed across the canal, and rose again as the load passed safely across. Up the other side toiled the camel, and safely "barracked" at its destination, when one thousand and forty (1,040) pounds weight of grain was removed from its back. Half a ton carried under such circumstances is an achievement which surely entitled the noble animal to the name he was afterwards always known by, "Samson."

At first the Camel Corps was supplied with Bikanir camels from India—big, strong animals of a dark, tawny colour, but later on lighter Egyptian camels were used for riding purposes. Early in the war the Maharajah of Bikanir is said to have made a princely gift of five hundred Bikanir camels to the British Government for the use of the army in Egypt.

The Camel Transport Corps, a different body altogether from the Imperial Camel Corps, was supplied with heavy draught camels for the purpose of carrying stores of all kinds from the base dumps to the various parts of the front line. In the advance up the coastal plain in Palestine, in November, 1917, General Allenby used thirty thousand (30,000) camels for carrying food, water and ammunition to the troops of one portion of the eastern force of his army. If all these animals were strung out in single file, head to tail, allowing twelve feet for each, they would form a column sixty-eight miles long.

Only male camels were used in the Camel Brigade. It would have been an unworkable system to have mixed the sexes, as in the East no mutilation of male animals, either horses, donkeys or camels for sterilisation purposes, is ever practised by the Mohammedans. The male camel, like the stag in its rutting season, is sexually excited at certain seasons of the year. When it is in this state, called " syming," it is bad-tempered and has to be handled carefully. Sometimes in the syming season a bull camel will go mad, and attempt to run amok through the lines, attacking anyone in its path. In this condition the brute lurches straight forward with neck outstretched, bared teeth, and foaming mouth, towards the object of his attack, and blindly stumbles over rope-lines or other obstacles in his path in his attempts to reach his victim. When a camel attacks a man he uses his teeth first, and then attempts to crush the life out of him by kneeling on him and pounding him with his hard horny knees. The Gypos say " Huwa magnun," (he is mad), and seizing a long rope attempt to trip him up by running the rope round his legs, which they then tie together to prevent the animal from rising. They then belabour the beast unmercifully with sticks " to drive the evil spirit out of him "—the treatment is usually quite effective, and the animal can then be led back to its place in the lines in a chastened spirit.

On one occasion, at Rafa, a camel suddenly saw " red," pulled the halter off its head, and started along the lines looking for a victim. A trooper caught hold of a pick-handle, and planted himself right in the middle of the track down which the animal was lurching with head outstretched and mouth foaming. Everyone else bolted behind whatever shelter was nearest, but Jim stood his ground, and as the infuriated brute came at him with bared teeth, he hit it hard on one side of the soft end of its nose which caused the animal to stop and throw its head up in the air. Again Jim hit it on the other side of its jaw, and then drove home the attack with a blow on the end of its nose. This was too much for the " gamal " which turned tail with its intended victim laying on with his cudgel to whatever part of the beast's anatomy was handiest. Many a military decoration was bestowed for a less meritorious act. On more than one occasion a " magnun " camel was shot dead just as it was overtaking a victim, sometimes an officer, sometimes a trooper, who was the object of its wrath.

Horses generally have a strong dislike for camels, but this dislike can be overcome by daily contact. Some of the officers of higher rank of each battalion used horses during part of the campaign, and these soon grew quite accustomed to the company of their more ungainly associates. This feeling of antipathy on the part of the horse was made use of in war in olden times, as for example, when Cyrus, the king of Persia, attacked Croesus, the fabulously rich king of Lydia, over five hundred years before the Christian era. Herodotus, in his History, states, " When Cyrus beheld the Lydians arranging themselves in order of battle on the plain (near Sardis, the Lydian capital) in Asia Minor, fearful of the strength of their cavalry, he adopted a device which Harpagus, one of the Medes, suggested to him. He collected together all the camels that had come in the train of his army to carry the provisions and the baggage, and taking off their loads, he mounted riders upon them accoutred as horsemen. These he commanded to advance in front of his other troops against the Lydian horse; behind them were to follow the foot soldiers, and last of all the cavalry. . . . The reasons why Cyrus opposed his camels to the enemy's horse was because the horse has a natural dread of the camel, and cannot abide either the sight or the smell of that animal. By this stratagem he hoped to make Croesus's horse useless to him, the horse being what he chiefly depended on for victory. The two armies then joined battle, and immediately the Lydian war-horses, seeing and smelling the camels, turned round and galloped off, and so it came to pass that all Croesus's hopes withered away." Evidently a camel corps had its advantages over horsemen even in those far-off days.

On one occasion in 1918, when our Battalion was moving down the Jordan Valley towards Jericho, on coming round a corner in a depression, we suddenly met a troop of Indian Lancers mounted on well-groomed, high-spirited horses, the riders with their picturesque Eastern dresses and lances at the carry looking very dignified as they kept their regular formation. As soon as the horses saw and smelt our mounts they reared and plunged, and upset the beautiful regularity of their ranks. The Indian cavalrymen looked anything but dignified as we lurched past them with audible remarks, not altogether complimentary, as to their horsemanship.

CHAPTER IV

HISTORICAL SETTING

New Zealand was represented in almost every major operation in the Great War, but no sphere had such a remarkable history as that portion of the Middle East in which the New Zealand Mounted Rifles and the New Zealand Cameliers campaigned, and in perhaps no other sphere were so many parts of the far-flung British Empire represented.

Viewed on the map, the Sinai Peninsula looks like a huge wedge driven home to its full length between the continents of Africa and Asia, with such effect that these two huge masses of land were split apart, the cleavage being denoted by the long strip of water known as the Red Sea. If this is so, it must have been some titanic God of War that drove it home, as this gigantic wedge has been the passage-way for forces of war as far back as human history extends. Across this peninsula have marched armies of the earliest kings of Egypt of whom any record has been discovered, over four thousand years before the birth of Christ. And since that time the sands of this desert have seen moving across them the armies of a great procession of Egyptian kings of some thirty dynasties— Assyrian, Babylonian, Persian, Greek, and Roman armies in their turn, crossed this desert, all bent on conquest; Byzantine armies, Arabs, Turks, Crusaders followed each other through the ages across these sands; Napoleon led his French army from Egypt to Acre in 1799, and after his repulse at the latter town by Sir Sidney Smith and his Turkish allies, retreated to Egypt over these same wastes. And now in 1916, an armed host composed of men drawn from almost all parts of the British Empire, took its place in the procession, and, driving before it a determined enemy, overcame the difficulties of sand, climate and transport in a manner never dreamed of by any of its predecessors.

These trackless areas had been crossed of old by Abraham, by the sons of Jacob, by the children of Israel in their exodus from Egypt, and by Joseph and Mary and the Christ Child.

The adjoining country of Palestine was the cradle of the three great religions of later civilization—the Jewish, the Christian, and the Mahometan. Here were their holy places, to these were directed the thoughts and aspirations of their adherents, and now an army which contained followers of all these three religions, was marching to liberate the land from the race that had held it in subjection for centuries, in spite of the united efforts of Christendom to wrest it from the hands of its oppressors.

The sands of this desert, unchangeable in the mass throughout the ages, but changing in detail with every wind that blows, have seen the coming and going of patriarchs and pilgrims, ambassadors and armies, traders and tourists, but never had they seen a host so varied in character and equipment as poured across them from 1916 to 1918.

Here were English, Scotch, Irish, and Welsh divisions of infantry, brigades of British Yeomanry and Artillery, Australian Light Horsemen and New Zealand Mounted Rifles, two battalions of British West Indian troops (B.W.I.'s), two battalions of Jews—the Royal Fusiliers, to whom a facetious student of heraldry gave the name of the Jordan Highlanders, and for them suggested the badge of three gilt spheres, pendant from a bar horizontal, and bearing the motto, " No advance without security." (The B.W.I.'s and the Royal Fusiliers formed part of Major-General Chaytor's force in the

Jordan Valley and in Transjordania in September, 1918.) Two companies of Rarotongans from the Cook Islands in the Pacific Ocean, proved themselves the best lightermen along the Palestine Coast. South Africa was represented by a brigade of Field Artillery, and half a battalion of Cape Corps Infantry. France supplied one regiment each of Tirailleurs and Legion d'Orient, and two squadrons each of Spahis and Chasseurs d'Afrique, while Italy sent one company each of Royal Carbinieri, Bersaglieri, and Cacciatori.

The names of the Indian forces which took part in the campaign are an education in the composition of the Indian Empire. Here were found representatives of no less than twenty-four different regiments. Squadrons from the Central India Horse, Hodson's Horse, Jacob's Horse, Poona Horse, Deccan Horse, Jodhpore Lancers, Mysore Lancers, and Hyderabad Lancers, helped to swell the ranks of our cavalry. Our infantry received additions to its strength from the Ghurka Rifles, Punjabis, Sikhs, Scinde Rifles, Baluchistan Infantry, Mahratta Light Infantry, Dogras, Kashmir Infantry, Guides, Kumaon Rifles, Deccan Infantry, Alwar Infantry, Gwalior Infantry, and Patiala Infantry. The Hong Kong and Singapore Mountain Battery added to the strength and mobility of our artillery. India's contribution to the forces of the Empire in its time of need was indeed a splendid one.

The military camp at Moascar near Ismailia in the Suez Canal Zone seemed to be a centre through which moved units or individuals from most of the " sideshows " in the Eastern Hemisphere. Gallipoli veterans were our comrades, men from Mesopotamia and from the " Dunster mystery " Expedition to the Caspian Sea were met here; troops came up from Aden, where they had some brisk and by no means one-sided conflicts with the Turks; some regiments came up from the malaria-infested regions of German East Africa, still carrying the effects of that dread disease with them; men who had taken part in the conquest of German South-west Africa in 1915 were with us; troops were drafted from Salonika to form part of our force. These were land forces, and all the time British vessels of war of all shapes and sizes, came and went past our Detail and Training Camp beside the canal, silent and grim, with never a word of their mysterious doings in the odd corners of the East, such as backing up the troops of the Sherif of Mecca, as did the *Dufferin* and *M.31* at Yenbo on the Red Sea coast; bottling up the German raider, *Konigsberg*, in the Rufigi River in East Africa; penetrating in the form of light-draft river gunboats as far up the Tigris as Bagdad and beyond; supplying explosives for the destruction of Turkish railway stock, and compelling the Turks themselves, who were within range of her guns, to carry out the explosions, as did the *Doris* at Alexandretta in Syria; clearing the Indian Ocean and Eastern Seas of raiders, etc., etc.

To an observer this position in the Canal Zone gave some idea of the vastness of the operations of the war, and when it was considered that all these operations had to be directed, and the equipment and supplies forwarded largely from the Mother Land, at the same time as she carried on the main war in France and Belgium, it gave one some respect for the brains that controlled the war machine, although at the same time, we freely used our privilege of grousing and criticizing the management, especially as regards such important matters as our animal comforts, food and clothing.

And along with these varied forces moved the Cameliers, mounted on the animals that had, for as far back as recorded history goes, been the natural means of locomotion in these desert places; and south and west

Camel Company Camp, Arnussi

Two Companies at Rhum

Camel Patrol in Sinai

Mid-day Halt.

in Egypt, and east and north in the Sinai Peninsula and Palestine, they carried out their patrols, and took part in all the military operations of the campaign.

CHAPTER V

THE LAND

THE northern portion of the Sinai Peninsula for a hundred miles east of the Suez Canal, and for an average breadth of thirty miles south from the Mediterranean Sea, consists of pure and unadulterated sand, rolling ridges in endless succession like the waves of the sea in multitude. Kinglake in the description of his journey across Sinai says: " As long as you are journeying in the interior of the desert you have no particular point to make for as your resting-place. The endless sands yield nothing but small, stunted shrubs; even these fail after the first two or three days, and from that time you pass over broad plains, you pass over newly-reared hills, you pass through valleys dug out by last week's storm, and the hills and the valleys are sand, sand, still sand, and only sand and sand and sand again."

An Australian trooper who climbed to the top of a sand-ridge near his halting-place to get a view of the surrounding country, when asked what he saw, replied, " Miles and miles and miles of damn-all."

The Sixteenth N.Z. Company I.C.C. spent the months of April and May, 1917 in the Sinai Desert, and these same months of 1918 in the Jordan Valley, some hundred miles farther north, and were able to note the contrast between the climates of these two districts. In the Sinai the sun beats down day after day from a cloudless sky, and the heat is radiated back from the white sand which grows intensely hot on the surface, but the heat in this arid area is not so trying as the humid heat in the Jordan Valley. At night in the latter place, the temperature did not drop to any great extent, and one would awake in the middle of the night, bathed in perspiration, whereas in Sinai the radiation of heat at night from the dry loose sand was so rapid that the temperature fell quickly, and when sleeping on the sand one would be awakened by the cold in the small hours of the morning. In a well-known song a lover vowed that his love would endure " till the sands of the desert grow cold." He evidently did not realize that he was informing his lady-love that he would cease to love her about 2 a.m. every day.

The greatest trouble caused by the heat in this dry area was the intense thirst created. The sources of water supply away from the newly built railway line were wells, which were few and far between, and the water obtained from these was more or less brackish, and sometimes worse. As the army advanced across the desert in 1916, a railway line from the Canal was constructed behind it, and a pipe line was laid down, through which was pumped water from the fresh-water canal from the River Nile. This canal flowed close to our camp near Ismailia, but the water there was of such a doubtful nature that it was made a crime to be caught drinking it or even washing or bathing in it. Yet this water, siphoned under the Canal at Kantara, was put through large filtering tanks and passed on in pipes from pumping station to pumping station, until in 1917 it reached nearly to the Wadi Ghuzzi south of Gaza in the south of Palestine, a distance of well over a hundred miles from the Canal.

This was the first time that the water difficulty in the passage of the Sinai Desert had been successfully overcome by mechanical means, but the idea is not quite a modern one, since Herodotus, who lived about four and a half centuries before the birth of Christ, tells how Cambyses, King of Persia, when contemplating an invasion of Egypt, made a treaty with a king of the Arabs. He states that " When, therefore, the Arabian had pledged his faith to the messengers of Cambyses, he straightway contrived as follows: He filled a number of camels' skins with water, and loading therewith all the live camels that he possessed, drove them into the desert, and awaited the coming of the army. This is the more likely of the two tales that are told. The other is an improbable story, but as it is related I think that I ought not to pass it by. There is a great river in Arabia, called the Corys, which empties itself into the Erythrean Sea. The Arab king, they say, made a pipe of the skins of oxen and other beasts, reaching from this river all the way to the desert, and so brought the water to certain cisterns which he had had dug in the desert to receive it. It is a twelve days' journey from the river to this desert tract. And the water they say, was brought through three different pipes to three separate places."

Heredotus must have heard these two stories not very long after the incidents were supposed to have happened, as he says that he saw and examined the bones of the slain on the field of the battle in which Cambyses defeated the Egyptians near Pelusium, after his crossing the desert. It seems strange that some two thousand four hundred years afterwards, camels and water-pipes should be successfully used to supply water from Egypt to an invading army marching in the opposite direction to that in which the Persians were going.

The pipes laid by the British during their advance were placed underground, free from the heating power of the sun, and the water was clear and cool, but in the opinion of the men in the ranks, the taste was spoilt by being chlorinated by the medical experts, and many were the maledictions called down on the heads of the latter, when the billy was boiled. But in this war the medical profession took no risks, and their actions were well justified by the remarkable results obtained. After the

Armistice a New Zealand medical officer—a Boer War veteran, in charge of the New Zealand Detail Camp, who had to examine every man who passed through it, told the writer that he had found only two cases who had contracted enteric fever during the Sinai-Palestine campaign, and these two men had gone beyond the regulation time between inoculations. When it is remembered that in the Boer War more men were said to have died from enteric fever than were killed by enemy bullets, and when the natural water supply in Sinai and Palestine is taken into consideration, wells, some dug in the time of Abraham, and never since cleaned out, the results are truly remarkable.

Officers and other ranks tried to obtain other ingredients to discourage the microbes, and to take the sting out of the local water, or perhaps to put another sting into it. It is said that during the advance across the desert, the supply of liquor in the officers' mess in one New Zealand regiment had run out, and the mess secretary was authorized to send a telegram to an officer who was on leave in Cairo, instructing him to bring back a case of whisky when he was returning the following day.

The secretary came back almost immediately from the signallers' department and reported to the mess that the message could not be accepted for transmission over the military wires as it was not on military business. Another officer at once said he would get it despatched, and the secretary made a bet of a hundred piastres with him that he could not. He went off and returned in five minutes saying the message had gone. Asked how he had managed it the officer said he had made it a military order: "Captain A.B., N.Z.M.R., Shepheard's Hotel, Cairo. Please instruct Reg. No. 1820 Sergt. J. Walker and eleven companions to report here with you to-morrow. Signed, C.D. Capt." and on the morrow twelve bottles of Johnny Walker arrived at the N.Z. mess—still going strong. Difficulties are made to be overcome, and colonials frequently seem to have the faculty of overcoming them.

Perhaps the greatest heat we felt in 1917 was on April 25, when the 16th Company was camped at Lahfan, fifteen miles from El Arish. That day the camels were sent to be watered at some wells five miles away, but when they arrived there it was found that the pumping apparatus had broken down, so there was nothing else to do but go on another ten miles to El Arish. The sky was covered with a peculiar haze through which the sun blazed down in a cruel manner, so that by the time the latter place was reached the animals were showing signs of distress. Fresh water had been discovered by the Engineers just a few feet below the sand on the sea-beach, and canvas watering troughs had been set up so near to the sea from them that one could throw a stone into the Mediterranean Sea, if one could find the stone. The heat rose off the dry sand on the beach as if coming from a furnace, and it was extremely painful to walk barefooted. Just as the camels reached the troughs one collapsed and died in a few minutes. After the animals were watered they were barracked down for an hour, as it would have been dangerous to travel them on such a day immediately after they had laid in their several days' supply of water. During this hour all hands plunged into the sea and had a bathe that still lingers in one's memory. On the return journey we passed several well-nourished camels lying dead by the wayside, and found on arrival at our camp that some of the pack-camels left behind in our own lines had also passed out. It was said that between seventy and eighty camels in the El Arish area died that day as a result of the extreme heat, yet none of our men on duty seemed any the worse for their experience;

some of us had to take our turn on outpost duty that same night as usual. To have to travel fifteen miles for a drink of water, and to return fifteen miles afterward in a broiling heat that would kill camels, gives a different idea of the value of water from that generally held in more temperate countries.

After the Wadi El Arish is crossed on the eastern side of the Sinai desert the country gradually changes into flat or slightly undulating sandy loam, stretching inland and fringed with sandhills along the coast. This flat coastal plain, the land of the Philistines of old, runs back from the sea till it merges into the low foothills which in turn rise into the range of the Judaean Mountains, some two thousand feet in average height. The plain continues north gradually narrowing in width as the mountains draw nearer to the sea, until they end in a high hill, Mt. Carmel, abutting on to the coast at the town of Haifa. This coastal plain is the most fertile portion of Palestine, and even under the crude methods of Bedouin cultivation, crops of wheat and barley were produced, sometimes with quite a good yield, but under more intensive cultivation with modern implements, the Zionist Jews of the various scattered villages had vineyards and orange groves that produced splendid yields of fruit, the quality of which, after our long sojourn in the wilderness, we unanimously declared to be the finest in the world.

East of the coastal plain lies the limestone plateau of Judaea, over two thousand feet in height, on which Jerusalem and Bethlehem are situated. The eastern side of this tableland drops rapidly into the great trough occupied by the basin of the Jordan River and the Dead Sea, the latter being one thousand two hundred and ninety-two feet below sea-level.

East of this great depression, the land rises very rapidly into the tableland of Gilead and Moab, now forming part of Transjordania. Here the soil is fertile and well suited for wheat growing. This district was once one of the sources of the supplies of grain for the Roman Empire, and in the town of Amman are still to be seen remains of Roman occupation in the Citadel and the amphitheatre which was capable of seating four or five thousand spectators.

In the country of Syria to the north of Palestine the mountains lie nearer to the sea, the highest peak, Mt. Hermon, over 9,000 feet high, carrying snow well into summer. The Jordan River has its sources on the slopes of this and neighbouring mountains, and is thus a snow fed river whose volume of water is well maintained all the year round.

In the Sinai Desert there is no town or village till El Arish is reached. Only few small scattered parties of Bedouins are to be found in some of the palm hods. In Southern Palestine there are very few towns, and villages are few and far between. Farther north the country lying near Jaffa is more thickly populated, as here are many thriving Zionist colonies. The hilly country of Syria contains a larger native population, the towns being on the coast, or in the inland plain between the Lebanon and Anti-Lebanon Mountains.

These lands must have been very densely populated in the earliest historical times. The Book of Numbers and also Josephus state that the Israelites at Mt. Sinai were able to provide " six hundred thousand that were able to go to war from twenty to fifty years of age," a force almost equal to the combined armies of Britain and Turkey in the late war in Palestine. In the time of Jehoshaphat, as recorded in the Second Book of Chronicles, the small kingdom of Judah alone had an effective army of one million one hundred and sixty thousand men. In those early Biblical times, and up to the time of the Roman Empire, the loss to the population by war and massacre must have been unequalled in the experience of any other nation in the world.

As a contrast, during the Great War, the Turkish prisoners were well treated in concentration camps, and well washed, well clothed, well sheltered, and well fed. The inhabitants of the towns and villages, who were usually non-combatants, had implicit faith in the British forces, and immediately such places as Beersheba, Gaza, and Jaffa were captured by us, the civil population who had left these towns during the attacks on them, began to return openly past our camps, carrying with them their household goods, and driving their flocks of sheep and goats back to the grazing grounds near their old homes. Perhaps an odd sheep might be lost on the way past, but sheep are inclined to stray, being sheep until they are killed, when they become mutton, and even those stray Eastern sheep made quite good mutton, and provided a change of menu from Fray Bentos and bully beef, but such occasions were rare, and usually compensation was given for the " accident."

Arabic was the language of most of the population of Palestine and Syria, while the officials of the government spoke Turkish. No encouragement was given to our troops to learn either language, and parties would sometimes be sent off on reconnaissances into enemy territory without any one being able to communicate with either Bedouins or Turks. When we were blowing up a portion of the Hedjaz railway south of Amman, a large party of Arabs came to interview the Colonel of the Battalion. He asked the troopers standing near if any of them could speak Arabic, but there was no response, when a tall Arab stepped forward, and asked in perfect English, " Can I be of any assistance, sir? " It was a doubtful policy in time of war, to depend for an interpreter on those on the other side of the argument when you did not know how their sympathies lay.

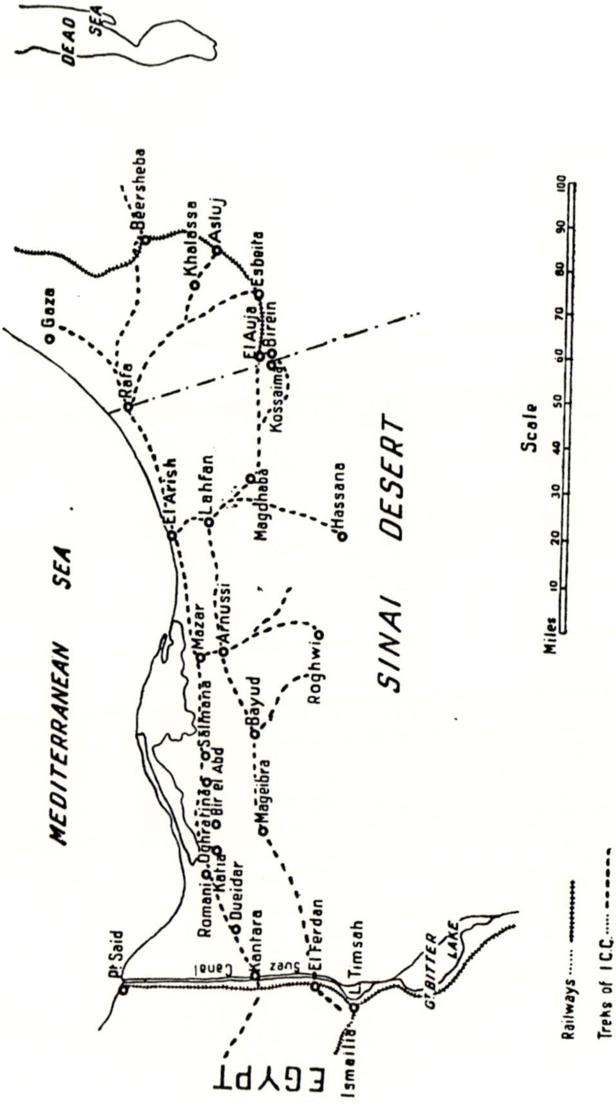
DEAD SEA
MEDITERRANEAN SEA
SINAI DESERT
EGYPT
Gaza
Beersheba
Khalassa
Asluj
Esbeita
Rafa
El Auja
Birein
Kossaima
El Arish
Lahfan
Magdhaba
Hassana
Mazar
Arnussi
Roghwi
Salmana
Bayud
Bir el Abd
Oghratina
Mageibra
Romani
Katia
Dueidar
Kantara
El Ferdan
Timsah
Ismailia
Pt Said
Suez Canal
Gt BITTER LAKE
Scale
Miles
10
20
30
40
50
60
70
80
90
100
Railways ......
Treks of I.C.C. ......

CHAPTER VI

THE SINAI CAMPAIGN

EARLY in 1916 General Sir Archibald Murray decided to deny the Turks the use of the three routes across the Sinai Peninsula to the Suez Canal. The southern and central tracks were rendered impracticable by the destruction of the water cisterns which collected supplies during the rainy season. It was considered that the northern route parallel to the coast, and said to be the "oldest road in the world," would be blocked if the Katia Oasis, some thirty miles from the Canal, were held by a mounted brigade with a division in reserve at Kantara. To reach Katia the Turks would have to advance over sixty miles from El Arish across a desert with a very limited supply of well water.

In accordance with this plan, the Fifth Mounted Brigade, consisting of the Worcester and Warwick Yeomanry, and the Gloucester Hussars, under the command of Brigadier-General E. A. Wiggin, was stationed in the Oases of Romani and Katia, some twenty-five and thirty miles respectively east of Kantara on the Canal. The Brigade was divided into four detachments which were posted at Romani, Katia, Oghratina, and Hamisah, with Headquarters at Romani, while a force of one hundred and fifty of the Fifth Royal Scots Fusiliers was stationed at the Oasis of Dueidar, thirteen miles southwest of Katia. No artillery was attached to these forces owing to the difficulty of operating wheeled traffic through the soft sand in this part of the desert.

Brigadier-General Wiggin, having received information that an enemy force two hundred strong was encamped at Bir el Mageibra, eight miles south-east of Hamisah, made a raid on it at daylight on April 23. That morning a thick fog enveloped the whole desert where the British forces were stationed, and this circumstance affected in various ways the four different surprise attacks attempted on that same morning.

General Wiggin reached Mageibra unobserved to find an empty Turkish camp, and not detecting the direction that the enemy force had taken, returned to Hamisah by 9 a.m.

The Turks from Mageibra meanwhile had reached Dueidar in the fog at 5 a.m., but an observant sentry of the Scots Fusiliers gave the alarm when they had almost reached the defences, and the defenders held off the attacking force until reinforcements arrived, and the Turks were driven back with considerable loss to themselves in killed, wounded, and prisoners. The fog was so thick that the Turks could not see the disposition of the British force, so that their fire did more harm to the transport lines than to the troops, fifty-two camels being shot by them.

At Oghratina, the farthest east post of the Fifth Brigade, the A. and D. Squadrons of the Worcester Yeomanry stood to arms at 4 a.m. when suddenly, in the thick fog, sounds were heard at the wells five hundred yards from the camp. An officer rushed down to investigate, and almost ran into a body of Turks. He gave the alarm, and immediately the camp was attacked by a considerable force of the enemy. Both squadrons of Yeomanry were driven back, but were unable to withdraw from the position without deserting their dismounted details. By 7.45 a.m. eleven officers and thirty-five other ranks were casualties, and the remainder were compelled to surrender.

At Katia the Gloucester Hussars stood to arms at 3.30 a.m., and were fired on by an enemy patrol that had approached through the fog unobserved. Later on a large body of Turks advanced with a battery of mountain guns which shelled the camp and killed or maimed most of the horses. The only officer to escape was Captain Wiggin, who was sent to bring up the horse-holders to the firing line, but while on his way to the led horses, he fainted from the effects of a wound he had received, and when he came to his senses, he saw the Turks rushing the camp. Reaching the horses, he hurried them forward to meet any men that might get away, and by this means about eighty of the force escaped, the surviving members of the rest of the squadron being captured.

When Brig.-General Wiggin returned at 9 a.m. to Hamisah from his raid on Mageibra, he learned of the serious position of the posts at Oghratina and Katia. One squadron of the Worcester Yeomanry was sent to reinforce the Gloucesters at Katia, and became involved in the same difficulties as the latter. Having watered the horses of the other two squadrons, General Wiggin advanced towards Katia, but also met with strong opposition, and seeing the British camp on fire, he concluded he was too late, and fell back on Romani.

From Turkish sources it has since been ascertained that the force that made this daring and successful raid, consisted of about 3,600 men with six guns and some machine-guns.

The Anzac Mounted Division was immediately hurried forward to Romani, but the Turks had retired eastward, and could not be induced to risk a pitched battle with the mounted troops. The 52nd Infantry Division took up and entrenched a position from the Mediterranean coast southwards past Romani, and the mounted forces continued this line so as to protect the railway which was being advanced from the Canal.

This successful raid of the Turks proved that General Murray's plan for the defence of the Canal was not effective, and stronger measures had to be adopted. It also led the Turks to believe that the British position was not invulnerable, and a few months later another attack on a larger scale was launched against the British position at Romani.

During the months of May, June and July patrolling and outpost work were carried out by the mounted troops despite the heat and discomforts of the waterless desert. The heat was intense, and this with the water difficulty imposed a great strain on the men and horses. In May one regiment made a reconnaissance to Bayoud, but the effects of the heat were such that on arrival at Katia, many of the men lay unconscious for hours in the palm groves. It is under such conditions as these that camels are more suitable for mounted work than horses, and so several camel companies that had been operating in the west of Egypt against the Senussi were attached to the Sinai force. A mobile force consisting of the 11th Australian Light Horse Regiment, the City of London Yeomanry, and three companies of the Imperial Camel Corps, was placed under the command of Lieut.-Colonel C. L. Smith, v.c. of the I.C.C., to operate on the southern flank of the British advance.

On July 19 Brig.-General Chaytor of the New Zealand Mounted Rifle Brigade, from an aeroplane located a force of Turks, which he estimated at over six thousand men, advancing towards the British position at Romani. This enemy force attacked the British in the early morning hours of August 4, and an all day battle followed, which ended in the repulse of the Turks, who retired day by day, from one prepared position to another, pressed hard all the time by the mounted forces. Thus one after another, the positions at Katia, Oghratina, Bir el Abd, Salmana, and Mazar were evacuated by the Turks, and by December, 1916, they were forced back to El Arish on the eastern side of the Sinai Desert. During these operations Camel Corps companies took part in movements threatening the flanks of the enemy, and gave very effective aid to the mounted forces.

Brigades of Australian Light Horse, New Zealand Mounted Rifles, and Yeomanry, took the foremost part in all this work. At first it was intended that the Infantry Divisions available, the 42nd and 52nd, should take active part in the pursuit, but this was found to be impossible. On August 6 the heat was terrific, and the heavily laden infantry men on the march to Katia suffered very severely. Out of one brigade about eight hundred men had to fall out of the ranks, and next day parties from the Camel Corps, Yeomanry, and Air Force were sent out to search the desert for these unfortunates who, when found, were frequently in a state of delirium.

The military authorities, recognizing the value of the Camel Corps for desert warfare, decided to add to the number of those already in existence by forming five additional companies from the reinforcements coming to hand for the Australian Light Horse and the New Zealand Mounted Rifles.

During the summer months the British army gradually forced its way eastward, and whenever it moved forward the desert it crossed sprang into life. A railway line, 4 feet 8½ inch gauge, advanced step by step, with a fresh-water pipe line composed of pipes twelve inches in diameter. This pipe line conveyed Nile water, drawn from a fresh water canal and siphoned under the Suez Canal into large filter tanks at Kantara, to the railhead for the use of the great gangs of Egyptian labourers who were forming the permanent way, as well as for the troops and animals all along the route. Railway stations, strong substantial buildings, comfortable huts for employees and military guards, reservoirs and tanks, were erected, and protected where necessary by entrenchments and barbed wire, while a novelty in the way of roads was constructed by pegging down wire-netting three or four strips wide. This it was found made quite a suitable road for infantry to march on, or for motor cars to travel over, but it would not stand horse or tractor traffic.

Night and day the lines of communication teemed with human beings of all nationalities, while railway trains, limbers drawn by horses or mules, and pack-camels in thousands came and went incessantly to supply the needs of an army continually advancing from its base. What a contrast to the usual state of affairs in this waste of sand, where the only sign of life would be an occasional small party of Bedouins trying to eke out an existence by gathering dates in the palm hods scattered so sparsely over the desert area.

But while this advance was taking place pressure had to be brought to bear on the enemy to discourage him from making attacks either frontal or in flank, and so in September, Major-General Chauvel with a mounted force of two Light Horse Brigades and three companies of the Camel Corps, with artillery attached, made a raid from Bir Salmana on Mazar, where the Turks still had a force in an entrenched position. The place was well fortified, and the enemy on the alert, so the attack was not pressed home. Shortly afterwards the Turks took the hint and withdrew to El Arish.

The Camels also formed part of another mounted force under Major-General Dallas, which starting from Bayoud, made two night marches, and attacked a Turkish post called Bir el Maghara, in the hill country some fifty miles south-east of Romani. The position was an awkward one to attack, the only approach to it being up a steep narrow gorge, and after forcing the Turks back from one position, the raiding force retired as the final capture of the post would probably have been at the cost of a considerable number of casualties.

CHAPTER VII

THE NEW ZEALAND CAMEL COMPANIES

IN addition to I.C.C. Companies formed from Yeomanry and Light Horse Regiments, two companies were formed from reinforcements for the New Zealand Mounted Rifles Brigade.

The adaptability of the members of the various companies of the Camel Corps was surprising when one considers from where they were drawn—from the crowded cities of England, from the Highlands and Lowlands of Scotland, from the townships and backblocks of Australia and New Zealand, many of them never having seen a camel before, and yet in a few weeks they became almost as expert in handling these animals as the Bedouins. The natives certainly were never seen putting their camels through the various performances that the Cameliers carried out—wrestling on bare-back camels, tugs-of-war, and egg and spoon races on camels, while the speed attained by the camels in trotting and galloping contests at sports meetings must have made the Bedouins gaze with wonder.

The Fifteenth Company was formed of New Zealanders under Captain J. G. McCallum, in August, 1916, and after completing its training at Abbassia, it trekked across country to Kantara, and then across the Sinai Desert to link up with the main body of the Camel Corps at Mazar, in December, the day before the army advanced on El Arish.

The Sixteenth (N.Z.) Company was formed in November, and after only five weeks' training, men and camels were entrained at Abbassia Siding bound for the Canal. The camels were led, coaxed or carried into ordinary railway trucks, where they were packed, standing as closely as possible, across the trucks, fourteen in each, with their heads tied down to the sides of the trucks by their halters. If horses or mules were conveyed in this manner half of their number would be over the sides of the trucks before the end of the journey, but the camels caused no trouble in this respect, and when their destination was reached, they were quietly led out of the trucks and barracked in rows alongside the railway track to wait for their loads to be put on. It takes something more than treatment of this kind to raise a panic amongst camels.

Sections of the Sixteenth Company were placed at various posts south from the railway line, and from these centres patrols were carried out daily to the south and south-east, to ensure that no raiding parities of Turks attempted to approach from the hilly country in the centre of the Peninsula, to threaten our main lines of communication. Such places as Mageibra, el Geila, el Geisi, Willegha, Bayud, and Arnussi, all mere names on a map, were familiar to the various I.C.C. units that patrolled this part of the desert in the latter part of 1916, and the early part of 1917.

The work assigned to the sections of the I.C.C. at this time was really that of flank guards, as they were peculiarly suited for this type of work. They were able to push away from the main artery, as it were, and, being a self-contained and extremely mobile force, were freely used for distant patrols, where horses could not be possibly used. An instance of such work was when a patrol of the 16th Company, consisting of Sergeant Wilson and sixteen men, pushed out from the vicinity of Mazar, their objective being (1) to locate a well or spring shown on the map as Roghwi, and to gauge the supply of water in it from the point of view of the number of horses it could water in a given time, should it be necessary to use it, and (2) to ascertain if the Turks were attempting to work through the Djebel

Maghara for the purpose of making a flank attack on our forces.

With a suggested four days' limit, this little party pushed out into " the blue," with little else than an ancient map, full bandoliers, four days' rations, and a liberal supply of the spirit of adventure. On the second day out, when crossing a range of rough hills, 1,700 feet high, they found they had missed their objective by about a mile and a half. The old map supplied to them was remarkably accurate. This map, incidentally was based on surveys made by the late Lord Kitchener as a subaltern in the 'seventies, and the leader of the party was able to locate within a few hundred yards features indicated on it.

In the rapidly falling dusk, movements of objects some distance ahead were responsible for a somewhat precipitate movement into a high strategic position where a very uncomfortable night was spent among sharp protruding rocks where both men and camels protested audibly until dawn. With the coming of daylight the " enemy " force was found to be no more than a roving band of Bedouins with their sheep and goats who were also making for the well of Roghwi.

Locating the well, the patrol found it to be one of the mysteries of this age-old mysterious country. A narrow entrance between the rocks led to a cave-like chamber some four feet high and three feet wide, the rocks on either side being like polished marble, made smooth by the passage of Bedouins, or their predecessors, whoever they were, probably for thousands of years. At the bottom of a sloping rock some twelve feet from the entrance was a pool of the sweetest water, which, when emptied to test its capacity, seemed to yield about twenty gallons an hour. One wondered how many people in bygone ages had quenched their thirst at this source.

Pushing away to the east through the Maghara Hills, the patrol encountered rougher rocky country. Steep cliffs, sometimes hundreds, sometimes over a thousand feet high, were seen forming a marked contrast to the monotonous interminable sandhills of Northern Sinai. Several traces of ancient ruins are to be found in these hills, showing that in the past this district was inhabited by a superior race to the few wandering families that are now found there. At another Maghara, near the coast of the Gulf of Suez further to the south-west, rock inscriptions have been discovered, showing that mining for turquoise was carried on there over five thousand years before the birth of Christ, by Semerkhet, one of the Pharaohs of the First Dynasty in Egypt.

It was with reluctance that the patrol, finding no signs of Turks, turned toward the coast. It crossed the range of hills by another pass where, for many miles, it was necessary to lead, and often even assist the long-legged mounts over difficult paths, often so narrow that the loads had to be readjusted on the saddles to clear the rocks on the sides of the paths, where one false step meant disaster.

The patrol returned safely to its base, and the sergeant furnished a report to the O.C. of the company, but this was much more prosaic than the reports issued by the individual members of the party to the rest of the company about the wonders of the land beyond the mountains, and the marvellous experiences they had encountered, which reports were, however, duly discounted in inverse ratio to the reputation for veracity of the reporter.

During this trip several of the beautiful desert gazelles were seen, and one of them was captured. These graceful creatures are most delicately proportioned, yet they must be hardy indeed to thrive amidst these arid hills, which are almost totally devoid of vegetation, of which the only examples noticed consisted of a scrubby bush, which must obtain its moisture largely from the night dews, and which no doubt furnishes a precarious supply of food and drink for these nimble creatures. The words of the Psalmist " As the hart panteth after the water brooks," have a fuller significance when one has passed through such scenes as these.

By the end of April, 1917, the whole of the 16th I.C.C. Company came together again at Lahfan in the Wadi El Arish, fifteen miles inland from the coast. From here patrols were regularly carried out to the south and east, and to Magdhaba, fifteen miles further inland. A reconnaissance on a larger scale was carried out when a party of two hundred Cameliers made a raid into Turkish territory for a distance of fifty miles, being away for six days without any vehicular connection with their base.

In May the 16th Company joined up with the Fourth Battalion I.C.C. at Abbasan el Kebir, and from that time onward it took part in all the movements of the Brigade.

CHAPTER VIII

FIGHTS ON THE BORDER LINE

IN December, 1916, a mounted force consisting of the Anzac Mounted Division (1st, 2nd, and 3rd A.L.H. Brigades, and N.Z.M.R. Brigade) and the newly constituted Imperial Camel Brigade was concentrated at Kilo 128, ten miles beyond Mazar. An attack on El Arish, twenty miles away was ordered to be carried out on the evening of December 20, and, travelling all night, the force arrived at daylight on the 21st to find that the Turks had retired without risking a fight, to a prepared position at Magdhaba, about thirty miles southeast from El Arish.

General Chetwode at once decided to surprise the Turks at Magdhaba, and ordered a force consisting of the First and Third Australian Light Horse Brigades, the New Zealand Mounted Rifle Brigade, and the Imperial Camel Brigade, all under the command of Major-General Chauvel, to march at midnight on December 22, for a night ride of thirty miles along the wide, dried-up bed of a prehistoric stream—the River of Egypt of the Bible, but now known as the Wadi El Arish.

This was a good try-out for the newly formed Camel Brigade (in which was included the 15th N.Z. Company), which received its title as a Brigade on December 19, as within eighty-four hours afterwards it took part in two night advances of a total distance of fifty miles, the capture of El Arish, a successful all-day battle (resulting in the capture of the whole of the Turkish force at Magdhaba) and a retirement of thirty miles to its base.

During the advance on Magdhaba the Cameliers found that the nature of the ground over which they

70

were riding in the dark, was in marked contrast to that in the desert with which they had been so long accustomed. Here the ground was firm, with scattered tufts of scrub growing on its dry surface, and as the column moved on steadily in the cold night, the unusual sounds were heard of the plop, plop, plop of the pads on the feet of the camels. The big brown Bikanir camels made good pace, and before daylight the bivouac fires of the enemy were seen in the distance, a sure sign that the Turks were not anticipating an attack to be made on them so soon after the British advance on El Arish.

The Turks had established six strong redoubts and numerous rifle-pits, with mountain guns to support them. The broken nature of the ground was wholly in favour of the enemy whose concealed positions were difficult to detect.

The 15th N.Z. Company of the I.C.C. had marched all night as a part of the Third Battalion and dismounted at 5 a.m. some four and a half miles from Magdhaba. The Company advanced in extended order as a dismounted attack, and formed the first wave of the battalion. The First Light Horse Brigade advanced along the dry bed of the wadi on the right of the I.C.C., while on the left of the latter were the New Zealand Mounted Rifles, and farther to their left was the Third Australian Light Horse Brigade, of which the 10th Regiment made a wide detour and attacked the position in the rear. The Turks resisted stubbornly, and by shell, machine-gun and rifle fire held off the attack all the forenoon.

At 1 p.m. Major-General Chauvel was informed that the attempts of the engineers left at Bir Lahfan, fourteen miles back, to procure a water supply, had failed. As the nearest supply was thirty miles away unless Magdhaba was captured, and as there appeared to be no prospect of an immediate success in the attack on the Turkish

71

position, the General reluctantly decided to break off the engagement for the sake of the horses. The camels on the other hand would not be inconvenienced by the lack of water for several days longer, which showed their suitability for raids of this nature where the element of time counted for so much in the case of the horses.

However, about this time the Camel Brigade in the centre with the Third Australian Light Horse Regiment of the First Brigade on their right, made a spirited charge, the former over a wide level stretch of ground perfectly free from cover, and the latter along the level bed of the wadi. With loud cheers the Cameliers rushed forward on the higher ground, while the Light Horsemen co-operated on the lower ground in the wadi, and although met by a strong fire they carried the position at the point of the bayonet, capturing the force of ninety-five Turks in the redoubt. This success turned the scale in favour of the British, and General Chauvel ordered the attack to be pressed forward at all points, with the result that by 4 p.m. the N.Z.M.R. and Third L.H. Brigades had captured other redoubts, and as the 10th L.H. Regiment had captured the Aulad Ali position in the rear along with three hundred prisoners, by 4.30 p.m. the whole of Magdhaba was in our hands with a loss to the Turks of 1,282 prisoners and all their arms, equipment and stores. The British loss amounted to 22 killed and 124 wounded. The 15th Company I.C.C. suffered a loss of ten casualties, all wounded, in this, their first engagement.

A small force of mounted men was left to clear up the battlefield, and the main body after watering their animals from the wells in the wadi, set out in the dark on their return journey to El Arish. After the long night march from El Arish and the strain of the battle the thirty miles return march in the darkness and dust, from Magdhaba, imposed a great tax on the endurance of all ranks in the force. Men continually fell asleep in the saddle, while their animals would wander off out of the line of march in search of something to graze on, but at length in the early morning of December 24, the column arrived at El Arish, with little energy left to get ready to celebrate Christmas.

Although not so mobile as the Horse Brigade on the harder ground our forces were to be operating on from now onwards, the Camel Brigade was able to take part effectively in the future operations, and added materially to the offensive power of the mounted divisions to which it was attached.

From Christmas onward, reconnaissances by the mounted forces were constantly carried out towards the east and south from El Arish.

On the border line between Egypt and Palestine, near the coast, the Turks had entrenched a commanding hill at Rafa about two hundred feet higher than the surrounding country, with the ground sloping away gradually from it on all sides. The country stretching to the north and south and inland consisted of a slightly undulating plain, while sandhills fringing the coast lay a short distance to the west; and the whole of this plain was under observation from the Turkish position.

The main Turkish army lay some twelve miles farther north, along the south side of the Wadi Ghuzzi, and the post at Rafa was an advanced one which would block the advance of the British army if it attempted an attack on the main Turkish force.

A night raid on Rafa, thirty miles away from El Arish, was decided on by General Chetwode, and once more the Camel Brigade took part in a long night ride, followed by an all-day strenuous but successful fight, with another long ride back in the dark to its base.

The attacking force consisted of the Anzac Mounted Division (less the Second A.L.H. Brigade), the Fifth

Mounted Brigade (Yeomanry), and the Camel Brigade, the whole force being under the command of General Chetwode in person.

The column left El Arish at 4 p.m. on January 8, and wound its way through the sandhills lying parallel to the coast, but by midnight the nature of the ground altered to a sandy soil covered with a light coating of grass, with here and there patches of cultivation which was much appreciated by the mounts whenever a halt was made.

Ten miles from Rafa a native village called Sheikh Zowaiid was passed, and all wheeled vehicles except the field-guns were ordered to be left there, a decision which later on affected the replenishing of the supplies of ammunition of some of the artillery and machine-guns during the battle.

By daylight on January 9 the force arrived before the Turkish position at Rafa. The New Zealand Mounted Brigade under Brigadier-General Chaytor was ordered to make a detour round the right of the position, to attack it from the north. In carrying out this movement the New Zealanders crossed the political boundary between Egypt and Palestine, and therefore were the first members of the British army in this campaign to enter the Promised Land, and to pass from the continent of Africa into Asia. In the battle that followed the New Zealanders carried out their part in Asia, while the rest of the army was fighting in Africa.

The two Australian Light Horse Brigades, the First and the Third, attacked from the east and south-east, the Camel Brigade from the south, and the Yeomanry Brigade from the west, while the New Zealand Mounted Brigade attacked the northern approaches to the position and cut off the communication of the Turks with their base.

Although the whole enemy position was surrounded the attacking force made very little impression on it as the day wore on. The entrenchments were well placed, the main redoubts dominating the country on all sides, while outer trenches with excellent fields of fire, concealed the position of the front line of the Turks who swept every yard of approach with their rifles.

The 15th N.Z. Camel Company had been transferred to the First Battalion I.C.C. in January, and took part in this action as a unit of that body. The men dismounted under shell fire some three and a half miles from the enemy position, and the 15th Company advanced as the first wave of the Battalion's attack. The whole of the Camel Brigade present had been thrown into the attack, and the troops, during the day, attempted to work their way forward by crawling or by making short rushes over the bare level ground. By 2 p.m. the advance was held up by severe rifle and machine-gun fire, and the position was being enfiladed from concealed positions on the right. During this advance the 15th Company lost its popular O.C., Captain J. G. McCallum, who had been in command of the Company since its formation.

All forenoon and up to the middle of the afternoon, the Turkish position was subjected to a hot fire from our artillery, machine-guns and rifles, but no impression appeared to be made on it, and at 3.30 p.m. the Inverness Battery, which was working in conjunction with the N.Z. Brigade, ran out of ammunition and was withdrawn from the attack. About this time word was received at Headquarters that strong Turkish reinforcements were approaching from the north from the direction of the village of Khan Yunus.

The supply of ammunition for the machine-guns of the New Zealanders was running short, and some guns were out of action on that account. Major A Wilkie, the Quartermaster of the Wellington Mounted Rifles, hearing of this, commandeered the use of the nearest cable-waggon back at Sheik Zowaiid, emptied out its contents, filled it with small-arms ammunition, and personally conducted it at a gallop to the New Zealand Brigade in time to enable the machine-gunners to take an effective part in the final advance on the main redoubt. The ammunition supply of the Camel Brigade, including that of the Hong Kong and Singapore Battery attached to it, being carried by camel transport, did not come under the order which held all wheeled transport back at Sheik Zowaiid, and so all arms of this unit were able to carry on during the whole of the engagement.

Well on in the afternoon, in view of the difficulties of the situation, General Chetwode, after consulting with General Chauvel, decided to break off the action, and retire, but before this movement was begun, Brig.-Gen. Chaytor on the opposite side of the position ordered the New Zealand Brigade to attack the Turkish redoubt, and with their advance skilfully covered by machine-gun and artillery fire, the New Zealanders swept across the open grassy slope over a mile wide, and captured the main redoubt. When this success was noticed the order for retirement was recalled, and all Brigades pressed on the attack, and one by one the various redoubts were captured.

The Cameliers had suffered fairly heavily during the day, but had worked their way gradually forward. The last forty yards were carried in one rush, and as our men approached the trenches the Turks held up white flags, and the strongly held position was won. The Camel Brigade here captured five officers and two hundred and fourteen other ranks.

The total number of prisoners taken at Rafa amounted to 1,635, while the losses on the British side were 487 all told. The casualties of the 15th N.Z.

Company I.C.C. consisted of one officer and two other ranks killed, and nineteen other ranks wounded.

For their conduct in this engagement two members of the 15th Company received decorations, Sergeant Trott being awarded the *Medaille Militaire,* and Trooper J. Marwick the Military Medal.

Darkness fell before the captured position was fully cleaned up, so a force was left in charge, and to act as a rearguard should the Turkish reinforcements make an attack. The main body then retired to Sheikh Zowaiid which was reached after midnight, and next day the whole force returned to El Arish.

The Battle of Rafa was the last major action fought on Egyptian territory. The British army had reached the border of the Holy Land, and henceforth the campaign became a contest to decide who was to have possession of the Land of the Bible.

Although the main Turkish army had been driven off the Sinai Peninsula, there were still small posts here and there which were a menace to the British flank or its lines of communication. One of these posts was at Bir el Hassana about thirty miles south-west of Magdhaba, on the central road across the Peninsula. It was decided to clear up this position, so in February the Second Battalion (British) of the Imperial Camel Brigade, and one section of the Hong Kong Battery were told off to accomplish this. The 15th Company moved to Magdhaba and stayed there in reserve while this operation took place, and then returned to its former camping ground near El Arish.

The Second Battalion left El Arish on the morning of February 18, and riding all night, appeared before the Hassana position as day was breaking. The Turks were completely taken by surprise at the unexpected appearance of the Camels, and the whole garrison surrendered; an armed Bedouin force which was attached

77

to it was also dealt with. One Camelier received wounds of such a nature that it would have been impossible to carry him back to hospital in a camel cacolet with any hope of his surviving, so a British aeroplane that was acting in conjunction with the force was signalled to, and it was able to make a convenient landing. The wounded man was accommodated in the observer's seat in the plane, and in a very short time was delivered safely at the hospital at El Arish. The air force thus added another branch to its service in the war; it already included combatant (machine-guns and bombs), intelligence, and transport, and now it linked itself up with the medical branch of the service.

Perhaps the most interesting raid, apart from any military significance, was the expedition to Mount Sinai itself, situated in the centre of the southern part of the Peninsula, the place generally accepted as the spot where Moses received the Ten Commandments and the Law. Here the Israelites had delivered to them a definite system of religion, a new moral code, and a purpose that were to lift them from their state of bondage, and weld them into a nation that would produce forces to affect the world's history, and that would persist in spite of persecution, exile, and the loss of its national home.

It was to this spot that a party of Australian Cameliers, fifty strong, was despatched early in 1917, not in the character of pilgrims, but to disarm Bedouins, and collect firearms that had been distributed by the Turks, and to restore the prestige of the British army in the minds of these roving tribes. Some critics unkindly suggested that the Australians were sent on this expedition for a refresher course in the Commandments and the Law.

Mount Sinai itself is over seven thousand feet above sea-level; its barren rocky slopes are exposed to the scorching heat of summer, and to the frosts of winter.

At its foot is situated the Greek Monastery of St. Catherine, founded, according to tradition, by Constantine the Great, early in the fourth century. This monastery, protected by its inaccessible position, has throughout the ages served as a sanctuary for anchorites, and persecuted members of the Greek Church. During its long history it has acquired a great collection of sacred relics, rich vestments, works of art, and a very valuable library of ancient books and manuscripts. Here, in 1859, Dr. Tischendorf, a great German scholar, discovered and obtained possession of a complete copy of the New Testament supposed to be compiled towards the latter part of the fourth century. This volume, known as the *Codex Sinaiticus*, came into the possession of the Czar of Russia, and after the Russian Revolution, into the hands of the Soviet Government, by whom it was sold in 1933 to the trustees of the British Museum for the sum of £100,000. It is supposed to be the second oldest copy of the New Testament in existence.

But the Cameliers were not experts in ancient documents, and although they were keenly interested in the display of wonderful paintings, precious stones, sacred relics, and especially in the effigy of St. Catherine with its vestments of gold, silver, and jewels, and as a contrast, in the charnel-house where are contained the skeletons of all the priests who have ever died at Mount Sinai, yet they felt they had to take all precautions that their pilgrimage did not take as long as that of the Children of Israel, and so they soon moved off north, following possibly the tracks of the Israelites of old, until they once more arrived safely at their Brigade Headquarters in the south of Palestine.

CHAPTER IX

THE FIRST BATTLE OF GAZA

THE Turks had entrenched a position south of the Wadi Ghuzzi as if they intended to bar there the advance of the British into Palestine, and Sir Archibald Murray made arrangements to attack their position, but before he could do so the Turks retired to the northern side of the Wadi, and took up a position stretching from the coast near the town of Gaza, south-east to Beersheba, some thirty miles away. The position was well chosen as it occupied the higher ground sloping down to the Wadi and the slightly undulating country south of the latter place. Several strongly entrenched posts were established which completely dominated the ground over which the British would have to advance if a frontal attack in force were attempted.

The Wadi was like the Wadi El Arish, a wide dry river-bed for the greater part of the year, with numerous tributary wadis running back well into the hills of Southern Judaea. Its bed was sandy or gravelly, its sides were steep clay banks, and its numerous branches cutting into the plain in all directions gave splendid places of concealment for troops lying in wait to surprise our patrols in this no man's land. Here and there in the lower portion of its basin pools of water lasted through the summer season, an unusual sight in this land, and these formed convenient places for watering horses and camels.

In the earliest chapter of the Bible in which cities are first mentioned, Gaza is one of the first six, and is the only one of those named there that has existed continuously since that time, a matter of over four thousand years according to Bible chronology. This town has, as far back as recorded history goes, been the key to the

Outskirts of Gaza

View of Gaza

Turks in Trenches near Gaza
(Captured photo.)

southern entrance to Palestine. It is mentioned in the ancient inscriptions of the Pharaohs of Egypt, when Thothmes III overran Syria about the year 1500 B.C. Since then Gaza has figured in every invasion by land, of Egypt from the north, or of Palestine from the south. It has seen the coming and going of the Pharaohs of old, of the Assyrian and Persian invaders of Egypt, of Alexander the Great, of the Arab and Turkish hordes, of the Crusaders, and of Napoleon and his army in more modern times. And now it was to see the holding up of a British army, composed of units brought overseas from the opposite ends of the earth—England, Australia, New Zealand, with representatives also from the great Indian Empire, at the same place where Samson of old gave an exhibition of his strength while in the prime of life, and where later, as a blinded captive, he suffered at the hands of the Philistines, thousands of whom he is said to have destroyed when he ended his own miseries by death.

Gaza is the only city that suffered material damage by siege during the Palestine campaign. Not only was harm done to it by the bombardment by the British, but the town was largely despoiled by the Turks themselves who freely used the materials from the buildings for military purposes in their defensive positions. The great mosque, Jami el Kebir, was used by the Turkish army during its occupation of the town as a storehouse for ammunition, and during a bombardment this store of explosives was detonated and the mosque was badly damaged.

By the end of February the British force had advanced to Khan Yunus, and the railway and pipe line were being vigorously pushed along behind it. Owing to the different nature of the country over which the army was now operating, wheeled transport could again be used.

General Murray decided to attempt another cutting-out expedition on a larger scale than before, and attempt to capture Gaza, and while the operations were in progress he established advance G.H.Q. in a railway carriage at El Arish. The 52nd Division (in reserve at Khan Yunus), one brigade of the 74th Division, the 54th Division, and the Imperial Camel Brigade were directly under the command of Lieut.-General Dobell, who was in charge of the whole movement, and these troops were at call, to be used whenever and wherever required. The services of the 52nd Division were not used at all during the attack.

The Desert Column, consisting of the 53rd Infantry Division, and the two mounted divisons, the Anzac and Imperial Mounted, all under the command of Lieut.-General Chetwode, was given the task of surrounding and capturing Gaza. The 53rd Division under Major-General Dallas was to attack the position from the south, the Anzac Mounted Division under Major-General Chauvel was to slip past the town in the open country on the east and invest it on the north, while the Imperial Mounted Division under Major-General Hodgson and the Imperial Camel Brigade were to watch for any counterstroke of the enemy from the direction of Huj or Tel esh Sheria in the east, where large forces of the enemy were believed to be assembled.

The infantry and mounted forces moved from their point of concentration near Deir el Belah, eight miles south-west of Gaza, shortly after midnight on March 26, and crossed the Wadi Ghuzzi in the early morning. Unfortunately about 4 a.m. a dense fog, unusual at this time of the year, rolled in from the sea and covered the Wadi and adjoining country. The 53rd Division moved slowly towards Esh Sheluf and Mansura, and halted as a reconnaissance could not be carried out till the fog lifted. Major-General Dallas had at first fixed his head-quarters at El Breij, south of the Wadi, and at 9 a.m. he rode forward to Mansura, and summoned his brigadiers and the commander of his artillery to a con-ference, but it was 10.15 a.m. before they assembled. By the time a reconnaissance had been made, and formal orders regarding the plan of attack formed and issued to the various commanders, it was almost noon before the attack was begun.

While Major-General Dallas had been moving his Headquarters from El Breij to Mansura, Headquarters of Desert Column had been out of touch with him for two hours, and as soon as communication was established Generals Dobell and Chetwode telegraphed him urgently to attack without delay.

The infantry advanced along two ridges to attack the hill of Ali Muntar, a hill about three hundred feet high overlooking Gaza from the east, and celebrated as the spot to which Samson of old carried the gates of the city when the Philistines tried to trap him in the town. The approaches were covered by Turkish trenches, and broken by numerous impenetrable hedges of cactus and prickly pears which gave concealment to the Turks and proved impassable obstacles to the advance of the British, who suffered severely from rifle and machine-gun fire and from shelling by artillery. The 61st Brigade of the 54th Division was thrown into the line, and the British infantry pressed on all the after-noon till by 6.30 p.m. the whole position on Ali Muntar was captured, but at a heavy loss.

In the meantime, in the early morning the two mounted divisions had taken advantage of the fog and had pressed on unobserved on the eastern side of Gaza. Soon after 9 a.m. the Anzac Division had arrived at its objective, Beit Durdis, five miles north-east of the city, and the 2nd A.L.H. Brigade soon extended its lines to the sea-coast north of the town. Squadrons were pushed out north and north-east to watch for the approach of any Turkish reinforcements, and one of these squadrons surprised and captured the Commander of the 53rd Turkish Division who was calmly proceeding into Gaza with a small escort to take over his new command. Although the mounted forces north of Gaza were under shell fire all forenoon, they did not meet with the determined opposition that the infantry did, and had not been very seriously engaged. About mid-afternoon the Anzac Division was ordered to press on an attack on the town so as to assist the infantry. This was done, and good progress was made in spite of the obstacles of cactus hedges and the resistance put up by the Turks in buildings in the outskirts of the town. When dusk fell the Second A.L.H. Brigade had reached the outskirts on the north and west, the Wellington Mounted Rifles (N.Z.) had captured two 77 m.m. Krupp guns and were in possession of a portion of the suburbs, while the Canterbury Mounted Rifles (N.Z.) had attacked Ali Muntar in the rear, and had joined up with the infantry of the 53rd Division in the eastern streets.

The Imperial Mounted Division having followed the Anzac Division across the Wadi in the morning advanced to Kh.er Reseim, north-east of Gaza, and came into contact with small bodies of Turks. The Imperial Camel Brigade had left its camp at Abasan el Kebir, five miles south-east of Khan Yunus early in the morning, and moved directly to its crossing over the Wadi at Tel el Jemmi in spite of the pitch-black night. It then proceeded to El Mendur on the bank of the Wadi esh Sheria, and took up an outpost line from the right of the Imperial Mounted Division to the Wadi Ghuzzi. When the Anzac Division was thrown into the attack on Gaza in the afternoon, the Imperial Mounted Division was moved farther north, and the Imperial Camel Brigade was brought up to Kh.er Reseim to help to resist the pressure of the Turkish reinforcements, estimated at over three thousand, which were advancing towards the city from the east. With the assistance of the Third A.L.H. Brigade, light car patrols, and two light armoured motor batteries, the advance of the enemy was successfully checked by nightfall.

The year was just past the equinox, sunset was at 6 p.m. By 6.30 p.m. dusk had fallen quickly, as it always does in that latitude, and by that time the 53rd Division had gained its objective, the dominating position of Ali Muntar, the Anzac Division had established a footing in the outskirts of the town on the north, north-east and north-west, the Turkish relief force from the north and east had been held up, the city had been completely surrounded except on a small section on the south-west, but General Dobell was not aware of the whole of the general situation till later on in the night, and as he felt that the relieving Turkish forces would menace the safety of the mounted divisions, he had decided that, unless Gaza was captured by nightfall, the troops must be withdrawn. General Chetwode agreed that it would be inadvisable for portions of the mounted forces to be fighting in the outskirts of Gaza while the remainder of the column was being attacked in force from the north and east. Shortly after 6 p.m. General Chetwode, with the approval of General Dobell, issued orders to Major-General Chauvel to withdraw the mounted forces and retire across the Wadi, and the infantry, at the same time, were ordered to retire from the positions they held. The Imperial Camel Brigade was placed under Chauvel's command so that it might assist in covering the retirement, and soon after daylight next morning most of the mounted troops had retired to the south side of the Wadi Ghuzzi, but the Camel Brigade remained to assist in the retirement of the infantry next day.

Later on in the night of the 26th, when General Dobell became aware of the success of the infantry, he instructed the 53rd Division under Dallas, to dig in on the position they had withdrawn to, and to link up with the 54th Division which also was moved back from the position it was holding. As a consequence the whole position gained on Ali Muntar was abandoned, but at daybreak it was discovered that the Turks had not re-taken possession of it, so the British reoccupied it, but a counter-attack by the Turks drove them out of it by 9.30 a.m. The British troops suffered severely in retiring during the day, and when night came they recrossed the Wadi Ghuzzi.

The total casualties on the British side amounted to 3,967, of whom 512 were posted as missing. The units that suffered most heavily were the 53rd Division and the 161st Brigade of the 54th Division. According to statements made later by the Turkish General Staff, the Turks' total loss amounted to 2,447.

On the night of the 26th when General Dobell decided to withdraw all the forces, the Imperial Camel Brigade hung on through the darkness, and next day had to fight severe rearguard actions. The G.O.C., Sir A. Murray, in his telegram of April 1 to the Chief of the Imperial General Staff in London, amongst other matters, stated that on the 27th, " The Turks attacked the 53rd and 54th Divisions and Camel Corps in entrenched positions. They were not in the least successful at any point, and again suffered the heaviest losses, e.g., Camel Corps nearly annihilated Turkish Cavalry Division. I estimate enemy losses 3,000 on this day. Cavalry and Camelry had to move back to El Balah to water, horses not having had any for twenty-four hours and camels for four days."

General Murray's messages hardly conveyed a correct impression of the true state of affairs. He stated:

"The operation was most successful, and owing to the fog and waterless nature of the country round Gaza, just fell short of a complete disaster to the enemy." And again: "None of our troops were at any time harassed or hard pressed. It is proved conclusively that in the open the enemy have no chance of success against our troops, but they are very tenacious in prepared positions. In the open our mounted troops simply do what they like with them." Yet our forces had to withdraw from the attack on Gaza, having suffered fifty per cent. more casualties than the Turks.

The Turks had a powerful wireless installation at Gaza, and another at Sheria where the bulk of the Turkish reserve forces were stationed, and as the day wore on, messages regarding the situation were exchanged between Major Tiller, the German officer in command of the garrison in Gaza, and Kress von Kressenstein at Sheria. The British wireless station in Egypt picked up all these messages, and as the key of the Turkish cipher was in the possession of the British Intelligence Department, the messages were immediately deciphered, translated, and telephoned to Rafa, several of them before 6.30 p.m., but for some unexplained reason, their urgency was not recognized at the latter station, and they were not received by General Dobell till well on in the night, and after the retirement of the troops had been for some time in progress. Evidently Major Tiller considered the situation of the garrison as desperate; by evening he had reported that the British had entered the town by the north and east, the situation was very bad, and his troop commanders refused to face the combat at dawn. By midnight he stated that unless reinforcements were sent before daylight there was very little hope. The G.H.Q.s at Gaza and Sheria had actually exchanged farewell messages, and arrangements were made to destroy all papers, and blow up the Head-quarters at the former place.

The various units of the British army appear to have achieved individually the objectives assigned to them— the infantry had captured Ali Muntar, later than what was intended it is true; the mounted forces had very successfully cut off Gaza from the north and east; the Turkish reinforcements were held by dark; the air force had supplied correct information regarding the movements of enemy forces towards Gaza; the Intelligence Department had intercepted messages interchanged between the Military Governor of Gaza and the Commander of the reserve forces at Esh Sheria, showing that both had given up hope of the town being relieved; and yet Gaza remained in the hands of the Turks, with no prospect of a second surprise movement of a similar nature being successful on the part of the British. The only explanation for the failure seems to be that there was a lack of necessary communication between some of the various responsible officers in the field and at Rafa and those in charge of the whole operations at Headquarters. It has been freely stated by prominent members of the mounted forces that if the latter had been allowed to push their attack on the northern side much earlier the result would have been quite different.

CHAPTER X

THE SECOND BATTLE OF GAZA

GENERAL MURRAY decided that a second attempt should be made at an early date to capture Gaza, so Lieut.-General Dobell prepared a plan to make a frontal infantry attack on the town, with mounted forces on the right flank. He now had at his disposal four infantry divisions (52nd, 53rd, 54th, and 74th), two mounted divisions (A. and N.Z. Div. and Imp. Mtd. Div.), and the Imperial Camel Brigade.

The 53rd Division which suffered so heavily in the first attack, was to move along the sand-dunes on the coast, the 52nd Division was to make the main attack along a front between Mansura and Sheikh Abbas, the 54th on the right of the 52nd was to attack towards Khirbet Sihan, farther to the right was the Imperial Camel Brigade, then the Imperial Mounted Division, and finally the A. and N.Z. Mounted Division completing the line to the north bank of the Wadi Ghuzzi near Tel el Fara. The 74th Division was in reserve, ready to reinforce the main attack of the 52nd and 54th Divisions.

The Turks in the meantime had greatly strengthened their forces and their positions from Ali Muntar eastward with strong redoubts towards Khirbet es Sihan, and Hareira, leaving no open ground undefended for the mounted forces to pass through as in the first attempt on Gaza.

The various divisions crossed the Wadi Ghuzzi before daybreak on April 17, and established a line of outposts preparatory to advancing on the main attack. On the 18th, the artillery on land and the monitors at sea bombarded the Turkish defences to prepare for the attack on the following day. On the morning of the 19th, the 53rd Division advanced on the coastal side, and after stiff fighting obtained possession of Samson's Ridge, and later on in the day occupied Sheikh Ajlin, but at a cost of nearly six hundred casualties. The 52nd and 54th Divisions which bore the brunt of the day's fighting were subjected to heavy artillery and intense machine-gun fire during their advance, and suffered heavily. Positions were gained and lost time after time, but by the afternoon it was recognized that the attempt could not succeed; one brigade of the 52nd Division alone had 1,000 casualties out of 2,500, while the 54th Division in killed, wounded and missing, suffered 2,875 casualties.

The Camel Brigade had come up from its position at Abasan el Kebir, crossed the Wadi, and had taken up a position at Dumbell Hill due south of Sheikh Abbas. Next morning it advanced on the right of the 54th Division, and the First Battalion I.C.C. (Australian) took part in the attack on the redoubt afterwards known as Tank Redoubt. During the advance a tank, used for the first time on this front, accompanied them, but when about a thousand yards from the redoubt it drew the fire of almost every Turkish gun within range, and the infantry and Cameliers in its neighbourhood suffered severely. The tank was hit several times by shells and finally burst into flames, but the remaining members of the attacking force rushed into the redoubt, and drove out its inmates at the point of the bayonet. They were now subjected to the artillery fire of the enemy, but they held the position for two hours, when hardly any were left unwounded, and the post once more fell into the hands of the Turks. The First Battalion lost very heavily in this attack, one company losing fifty per cent. of its personnel in a few minutes during the advance, but still the Australians pushed on, assisted by members of the 161st Infantry Brigade, about fifty all told reaching their objective, there to be further harassed by artillery fire and counter-attacks by the Turks, very few returning unhurt.

Farther to the right the Third Battalion I.C.C. (Australian and New Zealand Companies) also suffered heavily, the Fifteenth New Zealand Company losing its O.C., Captain Priest, who had succeeded Captain McCallum, who had been killed at Rafa. This battalion advanced across the road leading from Gaza to Beersheba, and took up a position on two prominent hillocks, but as a Turkish counter-attack forced the Fourth Light Horse back on the right of the Cameliers the latter had to retire to keep the front line intact. Months afterwards when this ground again fell into our hands the bodies of some members of the Camel Corps were found marking the extreme point to which the Battalion had advanced. In the afternoon the Turks counter-attacked in force along the front held by the Imperial Mounted Division, but this Division with two A.L.H. Brigades on its right, assisted by the N.Z. Mounted Brigade, finally managed to stop the Turkish advance.

Seeing that it was useless to attempt further attacks, General Murray decided to break off the engagement, and under cover of darkness most of the troops recrossed the Wadi in safety, the Turks evidently being too exhausted to follow in pursuit.

In these attacks our troops had to advance over bare slopes or ridges, exposed to sweeping fire from Turkish artillery, machine-guns, and rifles, while aeroplanes bombed them from the air. During the night advances the men suffered from the stifling dust, while during the day they endured the discomfort of the hot sun beating down on them, and the tortures of thirst, to alleviate which no provision could be made, during the attacks, to supply them with water, most of which had to be carried by wheeled or camel transport from railhead some ten miles away. If these conditions were trying to the active combatants, they were much more so to the wounded of whom there were over seven thousand listed as such on the British side in the two engagements, while in addition over two thousand were posted as missing, the majority of whom would be wounded, and who would have to endure their sufferings until discovered by the Turks after the retirement of our forces.

CHAPTER XI

MERELY A VISIT TO THE DENTIST

In April, 1917, after some months of patrol work in the Sinai Desert with the 16th N.Z. Company of the Camel Corps, Trooper " Kirk " felt fed up with the monotony of the life amongst the sand, piqueting, patrolling, packing stores and water, ticking-parades, etc., etc., when he felt he might be taking part in more exciting events in the front line, so he decided to have a change, legitimately if possible, but if this way was not possible, at all events to have one. When drawing stores at a railway siding one day he heard from some troopers in a passing train that there were rumours of a big move shortly at the front, so Kirk decided to go and investigate. On his return to camp in the palm hod, he put in an application for leave to attend the military dentist, somewhere up the line, for some pressing (?) dental treatment. Leave for two days was granted, and, supplied with the necessary pass and order for travelling, he set off in search of the New Zealand Mounted Brigade. Proceeding by train, he worked his way from one camp to another, till he located the Brigade at Deir el Belah. Reporting to the Military Dental Officer, he had some initial dental work done, and then immediately sought the O.C. of a mounted squadron, and requested to be allowed to take part in the " stunt " which, he had found out, was to start that night. Recognizing a relative of a former college acquaintance in New Zealand, and admiring the spirit of his visitor, the Major said he could fix him up as far as rations, equipment and duty were concerned, if Kirk could find a horse for himself, there being just then a shortage of remounts at the Brigade.

Kirk found his way to the veterinary lines, and accosting the officer in charge, he told the latter of his errand. The Brigadier happened to come along, and hearing of the request, evidently suggested that the "Vet." should do what he could for the applicant, so to Kirk's delight a horse was supplied. Making his way back to the friendly squadron commander, he requested that the latter should keep to his terms of the agreement. The Major, surprised at Kirk's pertinacity and success, agreed, and with the Colonel's consent, a place as Number Three in a section was found for the new recruit. The column moved off at 1830 (6.30 p.m.) on April 16, to take part in the second disastrous attack on Gaza. During the march that night Kirk let the rest of the men in the section clearly understand that he had not travelled all the distance from Sinai to act as a horse-holder (which is the duty of Number Three in a mounted section), and quite a heated argument took place. Finally Kirk's personality prevailed, and the Number Four agreed for the sake of peace, to act as horse-holder, and let Kirk go into the firing-line.

At daybreak the squadron reached the position they were to attack, and advanced at full gallop under artillery fire, thus forestalling the shells of the Turkish gunners, who failed to shorten their range to keep pace with the galloping Mounteds. When the latter arrived within striking distance of their objective, they drew rein, dismounted, handed their horses to the care of the Number Threes, and advanced on foot to the attack of the position. The Turks, with shrapnel, searched the position where the led horses were placed, and one of the first men to be hit was the horse-holder of the section of which Kirk was a member.

Kirk's luck held good during the three days of fighting that ensued, and he returned safely with the New Zealand Mounteds to the south side of the Wadi Ghuzzi.

94

During the day after the retirement the mounted men attempted to water their horses near Sheikh Nuran, but being under observation of the Turkish aeroplanes, they were systematically bombed whenever a squadron approached the water-troughs. When an enemy plane approached, the squadron would scatter and then, after the plane had passed on after dropping its bombs, the men would return to the troughs, to scatter again when another plane appeared. During one of these flights Kirk observed a bomb landing directly in front of a horse ridden by a trooper called Boyd. Horse and man disappeared in a cloud of dust; the spectators were horrified to see the horse completely dismembered, with apparently no sign of the rider. The query at once arose in their minds, " Has he been blown to atoms?" Such things had happened before, but out of the cloud walked the trooper, quite unperturbed. " Here, you blighters, fetch me a led horse. Do you think a fellow's going to walk?" he called to the astonished group nearest to him, and vaulting on to the barebacked horse, he coolly rode it back to the troughs to water it.

Kirk in due course returned to Deir el Belah with his dental treatment still unfinished. He presented himself once more to the Dental Officer, and received the treatment for him to be classified as dentally fit for military duties.

General Murray, in his despatches dealing with the attacks on Gaza, sets out three aims in the objective of the attacking force (1) to protect his railhead, (2) to pin the Turks to their ground so that they would not retire without fighting, (3) to try to capture Gaza, and having achieved two out of the three aims, he ordered the force to withdraw.

Kirk also had three aims in his mind (1) to receive his baptism of fire, (2) to take part in an attack on the historic town of Gaza, and (3) to receive dental treatment for a broken dental plate. Having achieved all his aims Kirk decided to retire to his own unit in the sands of the Sinai Desert, and become a Camelier once more.

His conscience, however, troubled him, and he saw only too clearly the position he had placed himself in, as his time of leave was considerably exceeded. He therefore took the Dental Officer into his confidence, explained his position, and asked the latter to give him a " chit " explaining that the extra time was necessary for pressing reasons. The D.O. rose to the occasion, furnished the document, and Kirk returned to his own unit in the palm hod. On his arrival there he was at once placed under open arrest for overstaying his leave. The next morning he was hailed to the Orderly tent, where his O.C. (who was convinced that Kirk had been indulging in a riotous orgy in Cairo all the time) gave him a severe reprimand, and asked what he had to say as to why the usual punishment for such an offence should not be meted out to him. Kirk produced the Dental Officer's certificate, and humbly explained that his dental treatment had been interfered with by the movements of the Brigade, and much as he desired to do so, he could not return without the sanction of the Dental Officer, and that he really was the victim of circumstances over which he had no control. The storm blew over, and he was dismissed with a caution, but that was the last dental leave he ever received from that O.C.

With such a promising start to his military career, it is not surprising that this enterprising young trooper should later on in the war be mentioned in despatches for gallantry at Amman in March, 1918, and also as a machine-gunner at the capture of Damascus, on September 30, 1918.

British Tank at Gaza

I.C.C. in Beersheba

AFTER the two repulses of the British at Gaza, our front line was established along the line of the Wadi Ghuzzi, except north of the mouth of the Wadi, where the infantry still held an advanced position along the sand-dunes south-west of the town. This line extended from the sea-coast in a south-easterly direction for about twenty miles across the undulating land to near the foothills of the mountainous country in Southern Palestine. Raids and reconnaissances were carried out into enemy territory, and all the time the railway communication with Egypt was being improved until there was a double line from the Canal to railhead at Deir el Belah.

The water pipe-line was also pushed on, and, with the improvement of local wells and additions to the same, a satisfactory supply for the large number of troops and animals was assured. For the purpose of water supplies and with a view to future movements, possession of all crossings over the Wadi Ghuzzi was maintained.

Training in the work of all branches of the army was constantly carried on, and every means taken to make the various units as efficient as possible. As events turned out, it was to be six months before the next forward operations on a large scale were to be carried out.

Before joining up with the I.C. Brigade, the 16th N.Z. Company was encamped at Lahfan some fifteen miles south-east from El Arish, and patrolled the country as far as Magdhaba, sixteen miles farther to the south. As reports had been received at Headquarters that a large force of Turkish cavalry was being concentrated in the low hilly country south of Beersheba, it was decided to send a small force inland to blow in and block up all the wells at certain spots so as to prevent them from being made use of as watering-places for a mounted force of any size. Accordingly a force of about two hundred Cameliers, consisting of the 16th Company with the addition of a number of Australians belonging to the Second Company, all under the command of two British officers who knew the country, left Lahfan at 9.30 p.m. on Sunday, May 6, 1917, and travelling all night, in bright moonlight, along the Wadi El Arish, reached Magdhaba at 2 o'clock the following morning.

To avoid detection from enemy observers from the air, the camels were barracked close up to the foot of the cliffs in the dry bed of the Wadi near to the old Turkish headquarters, the concrete buildings of which were still standing. Signs of the battle of December 23 were seen on all sides in the shape of shells and shell-cases, remains of equipment, pierced walls, etc. Mounds of earth here and there told that many Turks had here fought their last fight, while a short distance away a wooden cross marked the spot where a New Zealand lad and an Australian Light Horseman slept together in their last sleep.

There was one well in the dry bed of the Wadi, and here on this day two parties of Bedouins had come to water their sheep, goats, camels and donkeys, and to carry back to their encampments somewhere away out amongst the sandhills, jars of water as supplies for cooking (but not washing) purposes until next watering day.

Then was enacted before our eyes a scene which might have been the one described in the twenty-first chapter of the Book of Genesis, which, three thousand eight hundred years before, had occurred about a day's journey from where we were. " And Abraham reproved Abimelech because of a well of water." Our " Abimelech," clothed in much the same manner as his namesake of old, with his wives and children, had completed the watering of their flocks from the well, and had filled with water their earthenware jars of native manufacture, which were loaded on the backs of their donkeys and camels in panniers made from the coarse fibres of the leaves of date-palms. The party had started to straggle away homewards through the sandhills, while the pater-familias was coiling up his coarse rope, also made from the fibres of palm-leaves, and had begun to fasten on the back of the last camel a rich possession in the shape of an empty petrol tin, no doubt the spoils of war, when the modern " Abraham " appeared with his family and flocks from another direction. The latter seeing the rich possesion of " Abimelech," greatly coveted it, and straightway begged for the use of the petrol tin to assist him in drawing water from the well, which was about thirty feet deep. But " Abimelech " would have no dealings with " Abraham," and answered him scornfully, as a wealthy patriarch would be expected to do. Then the argument began, with their faces thrust forward and almost touching, their tongues shrilly giving utterance to their opinions of each other, and no doubt of each other's ancestors also, while their open hands, upraised and waving violently backwards and forwards, emphasized their arguments.

But the flocks of " Abraham " wanted water, not arguments, and crowded around the mouth of the well, the animals in the rear endeavouring to push their way to the front, with the result that a goat was pushed over the brink and fell down the well. With its mouth full of water the goat began to bleat loudly, and when its owner heard the frantic gurgling cry, he abandoned his argument, and ran to the mouth of the well. " Abimelech," seeing the way clear, gathered up his rope and petrol tin in his arms, kicked his camel to its feet and disappeared over the sandhills as quickly as he could.

The owner of the goat also had a coarse rope, and fastening it round the waist of one of his sons, a lad of some sixteen or seventeen years of age, lowered the youth fully clothed down the well. With the assistance of some of our men who were interested spectators, the youth with the goat in his arms, was pulled safely to the surface. That morning we thought the cool fresh water in this well was the best we had sampled in the whole of the Sinai Desert, but after witnessing this scene we began to think the water might not be all we had imagined it to be—some goats, in the past, might not have been rescued, even in this unhygienic manner.

At 7.30 p.m. on May 7 the column of Cameliers moved off just as the moon rose. After travelling about ten miles it came to a Turkish light tramway and a formed metal road which were followed for some hours. In the moonlight the column moved in silence along a wadi which led in amongst hills of limestone formation. A thick fog came on, and occasionally the white tops of the hills appeared like ghosts of real ones in the uncertain light. No signs of human habitations were seen, and no sound was heard save the swishing sounds of the camels' feet, and the occasional barking of a dog or jackal in the distance. Daybreak showed a small tableland ahead about eight hundred feet high above the flat land on both sides of it. The advanced guard divided into two parties so as to surround this plateau, while the main body proceeded to cross over the top of it. The country beyond was concealed from view, but when near the top edge the latter party heard the whistle of a railway engine, and all hands hurried to the crest of the ridge to find at the foot of the hill a cluster of buildings with a railway running to the north, and an engine and train of trucks with a party of Turkish soldiers and labourers at the siding.

Our right flanking party had been observed by the Turks, who swarmed into the trucks and the train at once moved off to the north in the direction of Beersheba. Our left flanking party had farther to go than the other, but it made a dash to intercept the train. On the hill-top the main body were interested spectators of an exciting race between the camels and the locomotive but the latter won, and an exchange of rifle shots took place as the train moved away, but with no effects evident on either side.

This railway line had been built south from Beersheba for a distance of forty miles as far as this point which was called El Auja, and construction work had been carried on for another twenty miles farther south, past Kossaima, a former Egyptian Border Police post just across the political boundary between Palestine and Egyptian territory.

The Turks had been in earnest when they made an advance towards the Suez Canal in 1916, but in contrast with the British system, their construction of permanent lines of communication did not keep pace with the movements of their army. Even after they were driven out of the Sinai Peninsula, they could have used the completed portion of the line as a means of supply to a mounted force which, under a capable and enterprising leader, could have threatened or even cut the lines of communication well behind the British front line, or at least compelled the invaders to use up a much larger proportion of their forces in guarding their right flank and rear in South Palestine.

The labour party disturbed at El Auja by the Cameliers had been engaged in pulling up the railway line and transporting it for the purpose of using it elsewhere behind their own lines. Evidently the party consisted of forced labour, as one of its members, an Armenian, concealed himself when the alarm was given and was discovered by our men. It was gathered from him that his home was in Armenia, and that his parents, wife, and children, had been massacred before his eyes, and he himself carried off to work in a labour battalion for the Turks.

At El Auja our demolition party blew up a well-built railway viaduct of eight spans, constructed of lime-stone, and also blew in the wells in the settlement. The route of the railway formation was then followed south to Birein, and on to Kossaima, at both of which places the wells were blown in.

Kossaima appeared to have been an important Turkish post on the road to the Canal. A splendid spring of water gave a continuous flow, the first of its kind we had seen in the country. A large reservoir had been constructed, and from this a line of six-inch pipes had been laid for some miles in a south-westerly direction. The railway formation had also been continued for several miles past the post.

Our party camped for the night at Kossaima, and next day set to work to make a landing-place for an aeroplane. The heat was intense, there was not a move-ment in the air, nor a cloud in the sky, and the rays of the sun beat down unmercifully. An Egyptian Sergeant of the Border Police force who had accompanied the demolition party, was standing watching the men at work, when he collapsed and immediately expired, evi-dently from heat apoplexy. The working party kept on at their labour until the landing-place was completed.

The patrols of our party searched all Bedouin camps in the neighbourhood for arms and ammunition, and confiscated all the supplies of these that were discovered, the result being a motley collection of weapons of all ages and types of construction, many being more dang-erous to the party firing than to the party fired at. One member of a patrol returned to camp with two old-fashioned pistols and a supply of hens' eggs, which he considered he was entitled to seize under the heading of " possible explosives." The breakfast of his group next morning benefited from the legal fiction.

The raiding party returned via Magdhaba to its camp at Lahfan without any casualties, having been away for six days, during which time it had penetrated over fifty miles into Turkish territory. An aeroplane kept in daily touch with it, and the only means it had of communicating with its base was by means of carrier pigeons, a supply of which was carried with it in crates on transport camels.

By May 22, 1917, the 16th N.Z. Company I.C.C. had joined up with the rest of the Imperial Camel Brigade at Rafa, and the whole force took part in another demolition raid, on a much larger scale than the former, on the same railway. The Anzac and the Imperial Mounted Divisions and the I.C. Brigade made a reconnaissance in force on the railway running south from Beersheba. The task of the Imperial Mounted Division was to distract the attention of the Turkish forces from the job in hand, by making a demonstration towards Beersheba. The Anzac Division had the northern sector of fifteen miles of railway line, including a stone bridge of eighteen spans, assigned to it for demolition purposes, and the I.C. Brigade had the remainder of the line as far as El Auja to deal with. This latter portion included a stone bridge of twelve spans.

The I.C. Brigade left its camp at Rafa on the evening of May 22, and proceeded south-east along the border line between Egyptian and Palestine territories. A hot wind was blowing, and the long column of animals raised a suffocating dust. After travelling for some hours the column halted about midnight, and word was passed down the line that a halt would be made for two hours. At once camels were barracked, and the men lay down in their overcoats beside their animals to get a short sleep. Almost immediately a second order came along to get mounted. There was a gap between two battalions about the middle of the column, across which the first order had passed, but at which the second order stopped, with the result that half of the Brigade mounted and rode on in the darkness, leaving the other half to slumber peacefully. At daylight the head of the column turned up the Wadi Abiad, leading into the hills, and a halt being made, the Brigadier found to his amazement that he had lost half of his Brigade. While messengers were sent back post haste to find the missing tail, the members of the head of the column boiled up and had their breakfast by the time the missing companies arrived. The march was immediately resumed, so that the rear half who had the benefit of a few hours' sleep went without breakfast, while the front half who had breakfast, went without sleep—there are always compensations in every position in this world.

The Wadi wound for miles in among the hills, and finally narrowed down, until the dry bed of a creek formed the only track for the camels. At length after midday the railway was reached at a railway siding near which there was a viaduct of twelve arches, solidly built of limestone blocks cemented together. The engineers got to work with their explosives. and did their job so effectively that only four arches were left standing. Several miles of the railway were also destroyed by blowing off several feet of every alternate rail on both sides of the line with slabs of gun-cotton. The force then retired, and an hour or two after dark halted for the night near the mouth of the Wadi Abiad. No one needed to be rocked to sleep that night, and for some merciful reason reveille was not till 9 o'clock next morning.

El Auja Viaduct, blown up by I.C.C.

Esbeita Viaduct, blown up by I.C.C.

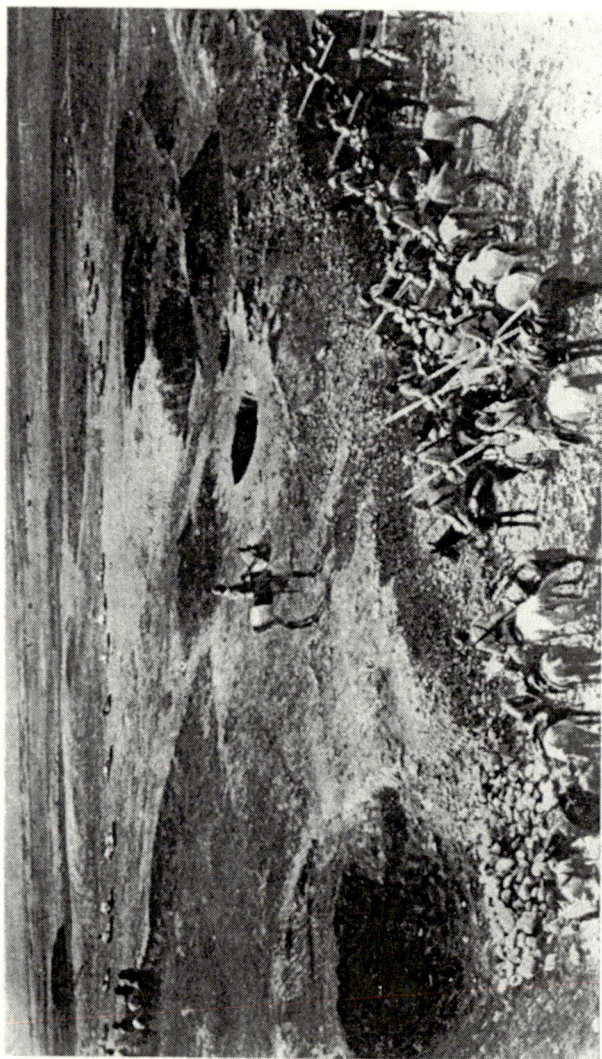

Turkish Cavalry near Gaza
(Captured photo.)

During the return to Rafa that day, parties of Bedouins were passed watching their flocks of sheep and goats grazing on the scattered herbage. Strict orders had been issued that the property of these people must not be interfered with, but that night at Rafa savoury odours of mutton chops floated about the New Zealand lines at tea time, but no questions were asked as to their source.

The district in which we had been carrying out these raids was the scene of archaeological surveys by C. L. Woolley and T. E. Lawrence (afterwards Colonel Lawrence of Arabian fame) in the early part of 1914. Captain (afterwards Colonel) S. F. Newcombe, who was in charge of the survey, led a raiding party of Cameliers on October 30, 1917, into the northern part of this same district behind the Turkish front line in the direction of Hebron (see Chapter XIV). Woolley and Lawrence in their book, *The Wilderness of Zin,* published in 1915, give a full description of ruins, mostly Byzantine, found in this region in the vicinity of El Auja, Birein, Kossaima, Muweilleh, and Esbeita, all of which were visited by the Cameliers in 1917, who by their destructive operations added their quota to the ruins in the district, which may prove of interest to archaeologists in the distant future. This district is generally supposed to be the position reached by the Children of Israel, from which Moses despatched a party of twelve representatives of the Tribes to spy out the Promised Land, and from which the Israelites were sent back into the Wilderness for a further term of wandering for forty years, before they again advanced into Palestine. Lawrence in Chapter IV of *The Wilderness of Zin,* states: " The roads running out to north, south, east, and west, together with its abundance of water and wide stretch of tolerable soil distinguish the Kossaima Plain from any other district in the Southern Desert,

and may well mark it out as the headquarters of the
Israelites during their forty years of discipline."

The Fourth Battalion I.C.C. (in which was included
the 16th N.Z. Company) seemed to get its fair share of
demolition work at different periods during the campaign. In March, 1918, it formed part of Shea's Force
which crossed the Jordan River, climbed under most
difficult conditions the steep rocky mountain slopes of
Moab to attack the old historic town of Amman on the
Hedjaz railway, and the Battalion, swinging round the
right rear of the troops facing Amman, ran the gauntlet
of shells and machine-gun fire, until, well on in the afternoon, it reached the railway between Libben and Kissir
stations.

A party of troopers selected from the Battalion had
previously been trained in demolition work, and these
at once set to work with slabs of gun-cotton to blow out
sections of alternate rails. Several miles were thus dealt
with, and the running of the Damascus-Medina express
must have been thrown somewhat out of joint for some
time after.

The noise of the explosions attracted the attention
of the Arab inhabitants of the village of Sahab, a few
miles away, and a large party of them, some on horseback, some on foot, and all carrying rifles, came over to
enjoy the fun. One Arab who could speak about as
much English as the writer could speak Arabic, had a
pair of field-glasses hung round his neck. I asked him
to " shufti " (show) them to me, which he readily did,
and I showed him mine. He pronounced mine to be
very good, and I replied that his were " kwaiyis ketir,"
(very fine). The latter were Zeiss prismatic glasses,
and on one side of the barrel was engraved the name,
" Capt. A. L. Gore, 1/8 Hamps. Reg." I asked the
Arab where he had got the glasses, and he replied
" Turkish officer, prisoner." As the Arabs had more

gold coins than we had silver ones, there was no use trying to buy the glasses from him with money. The only coinage the Arabs coveted was ammunition, but this we objected to barter with as we thought there was a big risk of our receiving the " change " in the form of lead if we happened to be worsted in our contest with the Turk. Some months later I met a Hampshire sergeant at Port Said when on leave, and asked him if he ever knew an officer called Capt. Gore. The sergeant said that Capt. Gore had been his officer, and three days after the Suvla Bay landing on Gallipoli in 1915 the regiment had to retire. Captain Gore went back to hurry up stretcher-bearers to get all the wounded away before the retirement was carried out, and was never seen or heard of again, and now some three years later, an Arab, some thousands of miles away on the border of the Arabian Desert was met with, using his field-glasses.

As the British were unable to capture Amman, the whole force retired once more to the Jordan Valley. The morning after we recrossed the river the Battalion was encamped near Jericho. Our demolition party, with the remaining supply of a few tons of explosives loaded on the backs of transport camels, was encamped farther out in the plain. Three Turkish Taubes selected this morning to inspect Jericho and its neighbourhood, and attempted to bomb the lines of the demolition party. One of our men told us later that he was never much in love with the war, but when crouching down between two camels, each bearing between two and three hundred-weights of explosives, with three Taubes trying to drop bombs on them, he loved it less, and he said he made a solemn vow that if he lived he would be neutral in the next war. If the Taubes had been successful in their aims there were nearly enough explosives to have increased the depth of the Dead Sea until it was over the

1,300 feet mark below sea-level, but fortunately the Turks missed their mark.

The Imperial Camel Brigade was reorganized at the end of June, 1918, the ten Australian Companies being formed into a new Mounted Brigade, the Fifth Light Horse, and the two New Zealand Companies were formed into No. 2 N.Z. Machine-gun Squadron which was attached to this new Brigade. The six British Companies were retained as Camel Companies.

In July, 1918, two of these British Companies, consisting of three hundred men, under Colonel R. V. Buxton, were sent to help Colonel T. E. Lawrence and his Arab army to make another surprise raid on Amman, this time from the south. The party left Kubri on the Suez Canal on July 23, and marched across the Sinai Peninsula, a distance of over one hundred and sixty miles in seven days, arriving at Akaba, a port at the head of the Gulf of the same name on the 30th. From Akaba they proceeded to a station on the Hedjaz railway, called Mudawara, which they surprised on the morning of August 8, and captured the garrison of one hundred and fifty Turks and all the arms and stores in the position.

Having blown in the wells and destroyed a portion of the railway line, the detachment moved north, their track being roughly parallel with the Hedjaz railway line. This must have been the route followed by the Israelites on their way north to the Promised Land, before they crossed the Jordan River.

The Cameliers along with their Arab allies arrived at a spot about fifteen miles south of Amman on August 20, when they were observed by a Turkish aeroplane. Their object was to destroy the railway viaduct and tunnel at Amman, and to concentrate the attention of the Turks on that position, so as to give them the idea that another attack in force was meditated. Unfortunately

Turkish guards were stationed in the villages between them and their objective, and as their force was not strong enough to make a direct attack on the position, a retirement was made to Azrak out east in the desert. Their last camping-ground before retiring was left well strewn with British bully-beef tins, and well marked by motor tracks made by an armoured car which accompanied the expedition, so as to confirm the impression on the minds of the Turks that an attack in force was imminent. This fitted in with General Allenby's schemes for misleading the Turks, and inducing them to believe that his next attempt to break through their lines would be on his right flank, as had been done at Beersheba.

Buxton's force made its way south again, crossed the Hedjaz railway, and passing south of the Dead Sea, arrived safely at Beersheba on September 6, having covered nine hundred and thirty miles since it left the Suez Canal.

When General Allenby's big final break through the coastal sector of the Turkish lines took place at 4.45 a.m. on September 19, 1918, the New Zealand Cameliers, now transformed into the No. 2 Machine-gun Squadron, once more took part in another demolition raid. The last formed of the Australian Brigades was said to have been selected for this very risky undertaking in a truly Australian fashion. The O.C.s of each of the other brigades in the Australian Division were said to have pressed the claims of their own units for the honour of carrying out this dangerous stunt, but the Divisional Commander said, " No, if anything happens to the demolition party, the last formed brigade will be least missed," and so the ex-Cameliers, the Fifth A.L.H. Brigade, with its N.Z. Machine Gunners, was selected.

During the lightning sweep of the cavalry up the coastal plain that September morning, the Fifth Brigade swung round to the right north of the town of Tul

Keram, where three thousand Turkish prisoners were captured. Without a halt except to water and feed the horses, the Brigade struck off north-east through the darkness, over the rugged limestone ridges, treeless, and trackless, but decidedly not rockless, to cut the main Turkish line from the north near Ajje, some *twenty-five miles behind the enemy's front line.* When the possibilities were considered, the remarks of the Divisional Commander could be appreciated, but the Brigade successfully carried out the raid, cut the railway, and returned to Tul Keram the next day without a casualty.

CHAPTER XIII

ALL IN THE DAY'S WORK

THE first rays of early morning had just begun to appear in the east over the low hills of Southern Palestine. A piquet of the 16th Company stirred uneasily in the sheltered " possie " he had constructed for himself from two bales of hay and some sacks of dhurra and tibbin. He had been on duty since 2 a.m., and although he had his overcoat and a blanket wrapped round him, he felt the early morning air decidedly chilly. I will not say that he had been asleep, neither will I say that he had not; the onus of proving the former was on the officer for duty for the night, and of proving the latter on the piquet himself, and as the former gentleman was sound asleep under his blankets in his tent, the piquet was evidently taking few risks if he did take forty winks, as the two hundred camels barracked in the line under his sole charge hardly even stirred all night long. But one bull camel had stirred; excited by his sexual passion he writhed his long cobra-shaped neck this way and that, at the same time slobbering a bladder-like sac from the side of his mouth, and blubbering with a hoarse rumbling sound, which showed that he had gone " magnun," or mad. At last off came his halter, and he lolloped along the lines in the direction of the feed dump. The piquet stirred uneasily in his corner, when his ear caught a sound that brought him instantly to his feet with all his faculties on the alert. There, not ten yards away, lurching towards him, was an infuriated camel looking for a victim. The sentry was unarmed, there was no place of concealment, so he fled in the direction of the bivvy-lines, with the brute in full chase. He knew that if those ugly bared teeth once got a proper hold of him, nothing less than death would compel the animal to let

111

go, and that broken bones and bruised flesh and muscles, or worse, would be the punishment for that short sleep at his post. Never did the soft sand seem to be so yielding, his feet seemed like lead, and appeared to sink deeper with every step he took. He could hear the camel's blubbering drawing nearer, so he yelled at the top of his voice for his mates to bring a rifle. By this time he was between two lines of bivvies, but dare not try to dive into one, as that would only place him at the mercy of his pursuer. But soldiers even if asleep, act more quickly than thought, and almost instantaneously (although the piquet thought it was an eternity) in answer to the summons, men in decidedly undress uniform with rifles in their hands appeared as if from nowhere, and the bull fell pierced with bullets, just as his hot malodorous breath fanned the back of the neck of the fugitive and made him feel his last moment had come.

The Sergeant-Major was aroused, and as daylight was appearing the order was given for all hands to fall in. A fatigue party was told off to remove the body of the dead camel and bury it, while the remainder of the company were marched out to a flat, sandy area and put through physical exercises and running practice for an hour. (The piquet was not asked to take part in these, he had had his physical and mental " jerks " in a concentrated form already that morning.)

Exercises over, three men out of every group of four repaired to the camel lines to feed the animals, while the fourth man proceeded to boil the billy for breakfast.

Egypt and Palestine being perfectly treeless, firewood was always in short supply in the desert, and what was supplied to the troops had to be brought overseas. Every camelier became expert in ways of finding firewood, keeping possession of it, and using it in such a manner as to get the last heat unit from it, but at the same time he was always willing to share his fire with his less fortunate companions. During a march, if a halt was made, and time seemed sufficient, no opportunity was lost of having a "boil-up." Each group of men always had a couple of empty fruit tins for making tea in. A man would secure, by fair means or foul, a piece of board from an empty bully-beef box or jam case, and would carry it on his saddle for days, or perhaps weeks, for use in such an emergency. Then during a "stunt" some day the order would be given, "Halt! Dismount! Boil up!" Then there would be a rush and scurry. Out would come the precious piece of wood, which had been carefully hoarded, and with a bayonet it was quickly split and broken into small pieces. The pint pots would be grouped over the flames, those of the later arrivals being accommodated round the outside of the blaze, and the bully-beef, condensed milk, and jam tins would be opened. Just as the water was becoming warm, the order might come, "Get mounted!" Imagine the scene, half a dozen thirsty men gathered round the small fire under a blistering sun, eagerly watching the billies coming to the boil (for the New Zealander and the Aussie do love their tea), and the hoarding of that lovely piece of pine-wood does seem to have been worth while. Then comes the fateful order to move off again. The water is not boiling and one cannot wait till it does, the precious wood has been wasted, the water is too warm to drink and too cold to make tea, and must be emptied out on the sand. Under these circumstances the war does not seem worth while, the sacrifice has been too much, and as for the "Heads" who were responsible, many a decent soldier forgot his religious teaching, forgot that he was in the Holy Land, forgot everything save that his carefully hoarded piece of wood had gone—for nothing, and that someone in authority was inflicting the cruellest form of punishment on a thirsty trooper. During moments like these there were invented new and lurid forms of abuse and blasphemy. But perhaps the water was boiled just as the order to move arrived. By some means the Camelier gets into his saddle, juggling and balancing his hot tin in a manner that would do credit to a circus rider. Then comes the order "Trot!" and he tries to drink out of the hot tin, but only succeeds in spilling the tea on his bare knees (shorts are a relief only in relation to hot air, not hot liquids), or on the camel's neck, which makes the animal plunge, and more tea is spilt, and finally, the rider's endurance reaching the limit, the tin and its contents, in a blaze of blasphemy, are hurled to the winds, while some cheerful idiot starts singing, " Keep the home fires burning," or " Another little drink won't do you any harm."

When in reserve the camels of a company would be sent out grazing after the morning meal. Four men would act as grazing guard, and as there were no fences or signs of habitation where they grazed, care had to be taken that the animals did not stray away among the sandhills and get lost. The halters were left on the camels' heads with the ropes fastened round their necks so that these would not get caught on rocks or shrubs. On one occasion when the Fourth Battalion was camped on a level piece of stony ground just below Bethlehem, the camels were brought in from grazing on the rocky limestone ridges near at hand. One bluish-coloured bull had arrived as a remount only a few days before, and was looked on with suspicion as being a bad character. Of course this particular beast this day had to have his rope caught in a crack in a rock, which pulled off his halter, and when he arrived in camp his owner had difficulty in catching him. Another Camelier went to help him, and going up on the off side of the beast, got his hands on him, worked his way quietly forward, and put the thong of his riding-whip round the animal's neck.

Suddenly the brute swerved his neck round, and with his teeth caught the trooper's tunic at the back of the shoulder. The trooper pulled back as violently as he could, but tripped over a stone and fell on his back on the ground, thus tearing his tunic away from the camel's teeth. The brute instantly came at him again as he lay on his back, and seized him by the arm. He used his heels to beat a tattoo on the animal's nose, while his mates pelted it with rocks of which, fortunately, there was a plentiful supply all around. The camel was driven off, but the Camelier had a brand on his arm that will be with him all his life. That evening the Battalion saddled up and proceeded past Jerusalem, wound its way down past the Garden of Gethsemane, and travelling all night, arrived on the hilltops overlooking the Jordan Valley. In the morning the Camelier went to the doctor's assistant to get some ointment for his arm, when it was found that his shoulder was a mass of bruises of a blue and greenish tinge, caused by the teeth of the camel when it seized hold of him, thus accounting for his stiffness during the all-night trek, but this did not deter him from taking part in the stirring times of the next fourteen days.

When the camels were being driven home in the late afternoons from their grazing grounds, they would disturb the insect life in the short, scanty herbage, and at certain times of the year it was a pretty sight to see the swallows skimming low to catch the small moths and other insects as they rose from the vegetation. These birds would accompany the herds of camels right to the camp, flying through the mob, swerving quickly to avoid the animals, but seizing their prey with unerring aim, and were never seen to settle on ground or shrub. Starlings, too, were sometimes seen in the evenings in great flocks, wheeling and counter-wheeling in the sky, with the rays of the setting sun lighting up the sheen of their feathers which seemed to be everchanging in their shades as the rays of light fell on them from different angles.

When the camels were once more tied up in their lines in the evenings, grooming and " ticking " would be carried out. The ticks appeared to be the same as are found on sheep, and were frequently seen on the surface of the sandy soil, so it was no wonder that the camels collected them. They concealed themselves in the wrinkles in the skin in various parts of the camel's body, and also in the split between the pads of its feet. These pests had to be picked off individually, and were collected in a tin and afterwards incinerated. Interest was lent to these ticking parades by Cameliers laying bets as to whose animal would provide the record number of ticks for the day. A wrinkled old bull was quite a safe bet for its owner, but even in these competitions instances of " crooked running " were not unknown; ticks were sometimes left untouched on a camel intentionally so as to provide a credit balance to be carried forward to the next day's total, and then heavy sums, for a Camelier, were staked on the result. But these tricks did not always succeed as other duties frequently interfered with the ticking operations, and the camel was left to carry his overload of parasites. It was the ticks that won on these occasions.

One day in June, 1917, when the Brigade was in reserve at Sheikh Nuran, the Fourth Battalion had a holiday trip to the seaside to bathe the *camels*. Reveille was at 2.30 a.m.; a cup of tea had been promised us before we started, but appeared just as we were ready to move off, and only a few were lucky enough to swallow it before the order to march was given. Daylight was just beginning to appear as the Battalion left its camping ground, leaving the members of the Third

Battalion still wrapped in slumber. The unlucky non-tea drinkers in our outfit felt inclined to envy the sleeping camp, but in those days one never knew what was in store for us during the next twenty-four hours. A fifteen mile ride brought us to the beach beyond Rafa, and then we were at liberty to enjoy our breakfast. The day was calm and cloudless, the blue waters of the Mediterranean lapped up gently on the beautiful shelving beach, and stretched away to the horizon. All the discomforts of the sands of the desert were forgotten in the anticipations of a plunge in the cool, clear water. But the camels thought otherwise. Many of them no doubt had never seen so much water before, and probably thought they had come to the camels' paradise, but when their riders tried to lead them into it, they rebelled; this seemed sacrilege to them to plunge their bodies into an element, which, from their limited experience, they knew was used only for drinking. So force had to be used. With one naked Camelier pulling at the halter, two or more similarly unclad joined hands behind each animal, and forcibly launched each " ship of the desert " into the watery main. No bottles of champagne were broken, and the speeches were short and crisp and to the point, but not intended for publication. When the camels got over the novelty of the strange element, they appeared to enjoy it. They looked very odd with their sheep-like heads sticking up on top of their long thin necks above the surface of the water, with what looked like an isolated round islet a couple of yards away, with a marooned Camelier clinging to it. Viewed from above, one camel in such surroundings must have looked like a plesiosaurus, or some other prehistoric monster, but a whole battalion in the sea would lead an observer in the air to fear that his reason had fled; the sight would be too much for his credulity.

After a very pleasant midsummer day at the seaside a return was made to camp at Sheikh Nuran which was reached at 6.30 p.m., when it was found that the Third Battalion had had visitors of a most unpleasant kind. A number of camels had been lined up at Headquarters for inspection to decide which should be put on the sick-lines, and which evacuated to the camel hospital, when out of the sky swooped an enemy aeroplane which emptied its cargo of bombs right in the midst of the assembled camels, and effectively solved the problem of the Veterinary Officer by putting twenty-six animals on the list of " Killed in action." Other poor brutes not killed outright were frightfully maimed, some of these wandering aimlessly around until overcome, when they either lay down and expired, or were mercifully shot. Unfortunately two men were killed and nineteen wounded. The Fourth Battalion was in luck's way that day, even if all hands did not get their early morning cup of tea.

The Turkish Taubes paid frequent visits to our lines about this time, and after such an experience as that just described, they became, in the words of the Irish Camelier, " a nightmare to us in the daytime." After this every man had to have a " funk-hole " dug in front of his bivvy, and each time a Taube appeared all hands had to dive for their underground shelter; they did not need much drill to perfect themselves in this movement.

A few Egyptians or Sudanese were sometimes attached to the Camel Companies to help with sick camels, and clean up the lines, etc. One faithful old Soudanese called Hassan, was a very friendly soul. One day he came to our Veterinary Sergeant and asked him for some medicine " to cure his sick eyes." " You should go to the doctor, Hassan, he will cure you," said the

V.S. "But I go to the Doctor, Sergeant-Major," replied Hassan, who never offended anyone by understating his rank, "and he say, 'Go to the Medical Orderly,' and I go to the Medical Orderly and tell him I have sick eyes, and will he please give me medicine to cure them, and the Medical Orderly say, 'Go to the Devil,' so Sergeant-Major I have come to you." The V.S. accepted the unconscious doubtful compliment, gave Hassan some boracic ointment to apply to his eyes, and sent him off. A few days later an inspection of the Brigade was held by the General, and during the march past, Hassan rushed up to the Veterinary Sergeant in the column, caught him by the arm, and said earnestly, "Look, Sergeant-Major, my eyes quite well now, thank you very much, you very good doctor." Hassan evidently believed in giving the Devil his due.

CHAPTER XIV

BEERSHEBA TO JAFFA

In June, 1917, General Sir A. Murray was recalled to England and General Sir E. H. Allenby was sent out to succeed him as Commander of the Egyptian Expeditionary Force.

The new Commander at once set to work to obtain a personal knowledge of all units under his command. He moved Headquarters from Cairo to the field near the front line, and soon produced a feeling of confidence in the minds of all ranks in the field. All Divisions were brought up to strength, and additional artillery and more efficient aeroplanes strengthened these departments of the army.

The mounted forces, consisting of three divisions, and the Imperial Camel Brigade, were formed into one body, known as Desert Mounted Corps, under the command of Lieut.-General Sir H. Chauvel.

The 20th Corps, under Lieut.-General Sir P. Chetwode, consisted of four Infantry Divisions, the 10th, 53rd, 60th, and 74th; while the 21st Corps, under Lieut.-General Sir E. Bulfin, was composed of the 52nd, 54th, and 74th Infantry Divisions.

The First Battalion (Australian) of the Imperial Camel Brigade, which had suffered very severely in the attacks on Gaza, was sent down to the Canal Zone, where it was brought up to strength, and carried out patrol work until it rejoined the Brigade in January, 1918. The 15th N.Z. Company was transferred from the Third Battalion to the Fourth Battalion in the month of August, and during the next few months the two New Zealand Companies took their share of the training exercises and patrols of the Camel Brigade.

*General
Sir E. H. H. Allenby,
C.-in-C., E.E.F.*

*Lieut.-General Sir H. G. Chauvel,
G.O.C. Desert Mounted Corps*

Brig.-General C. L. Smith, V.C. (Left),
O.C. Imperial Camel Brigade

During this period of preparation for the next big move, the enemy's land forces were content with strengthening and holding their front line, but their air force was fairly active, and their aeroplanes paid regular visits over our lines, which they bombed freely until our improved air force finally more than held its own against them. Fights in the air over our territory were frequently seen, and at length the successes of our airmen in most of these later contests helped to instil further confidence in the minds of all ranks who were interested spectators.

General Allenby's plan was first to capture the small town of Beersheba on the eastern end of the enemy's front line, where there was a good supply of water in wells, which were the cause of strife even in the times of the Patriarchs. The mounted forces were to carry out this operation from the east, while the 20th Corps was to bring pressure to bear on the part of the Turkish line extending from Beersheba westward to Tel esh Sheria. When this portion of the line had been broken, the mounted forces were then to pour through and pursue the retreating enemy, while threatening at the same time to cut off the Turkish forces in the vicinity of Gaza on the right of their line. The 21st Corps occupied the position opposite Gaza on the left of the British line, and at an opportune time was to press home an attack on the Turkish position there.

As in all this region there is not a running stream of water, every movement of these forces was determined by the water supply. To help to supply the requirements of the army on our right, branch railway lines were pushed out to the east from Rafa on the main line. In all railway construction the earthwork formation was carried out by bodies of the Egyptian Labour Corps under the superintendence of a staff of British Engineers, and excellent work was done by this

121

branch of the service. On one occasion when members of the 16th Company I.C.C. were going to water their camels at the Wadi Ghuzzi, they saw a line of Egyptians of the Labour Corps carrying sleepers and rails from a ballast train, and laying them on the prepared ground ahead of the engine. The material was put into position and spiked together by British engineers, and all the time the train moved slowly forward without once stopping. When the party returned from watering two hours later the train was nowhere to be seen, but a complete railway line disappeared over a rise in the distance.

The branch lines enabled water, provisions and ammunition to be concentrated at various points behind the army, ready to be carried forward by motor, horse, or camel transport as soon as the advance began. General Allenby, in his despatches, said, " Practically the whole of the transport available in the force, including 30,000 pack-camels, had to be allotted to one portion of the eastern force to enable it to be kept supplied with food, water, and ammunition at a distance of fifteen to twenty-one miles in advance of railhead." Allowing twelve feet for each camel, the above force, if placed in single file, would be sixty-eight miles long.

Increased supplies of water were required large enough to satisfy the requirements of two mounted divisions, preparatory to making a surprise attack on Beersheba. Two jumping-off points were chosen, Khalasa and Asluj, about twenty-five and thirty miles from the point of attack, and on October 23 the I.C. Brigade moved to Abu Ghalyun and Khalasa where new wells were dug and a number of old ones cleared out, some of which were over a hundred feet deep, and which had been blown in by the Turks to prevent their being used by the British. The Camel Corps erected watering-troughs, and installed pumping plant in preparation for the needs of the mounted forces, and then withdrew to the line of the Wadi Ghuzzi to take its share in the attack on Beersheba from another angle.

While these preparations were being made our improved air force prevented the enemy's planes from closely inspecting the country behind our front line. Movements of troops by day were kept down to a minimum, and any that were apparent to the enemy were of such a nature as to lead him to suspect that our main attack was once more to be made on the Gaza sector. By night, however, columns of all kinds moved forward in preparation for the advance. Transport columns established dumps of all kinds in advanced positions, and the whole country, after dark, appeared like a gigantic ant colony on the move. The transport column of Desert Mounted Corps alone, on the night of October 28, was fully six miles long.

All sorts of devices were used to deceive the Turks of our real intentions. A British Staff Officer staged a simple ruse in No Man's Land early in October. He rode out with a small escort as if on reconnaissance, and, when fired on by a Turkish patrol, he apparently collapsed on his horse as if wounded, at the same time dropping some of his equipment and a " doped " haversack smeared with fresh blood (obtained from a scratch on his horse's neck) and containing papers with " valuable " information in them. Along with letters of a strictly private character, some of them commenting unfavourably on the plans of Headquarters, and a roll of pound notes to lend reality to the " bait," there were copies of the proposals (?) to be discussed at a conference of Senior Officers at British Headquarters, showing that Gaza was again going to be attacked, backed up by a landing farther up the coast, with a feint attack by mounted forces on Beersheba. The Turkish patrol followed the party during its retirement, but when the " wounded " officer noticed that the pursuers had stopped at the spot where he had been "hit," he "recovered" sufficiently to escape in safety. To add more reality to the ruse, Routine Orders of Desert Mounted Corps, a few days afterwards stated that a valuable packet had been lost, and asked the finder to return it to Headquarters. Another party patrolling the same ground a day or two later wrapped up a lunch in a copy of these orders, and when an enemy patrol appeared this was also dropped to fall into the hands of the Turks. After the capture of Gaza it was found in Turkish Orders that a non-commissioned officer had been rewarded for discovering valuable enemy documents while patrolling, and also that all ranks were solemnly warned against foolishly carrying documents containing information likely to be of use to the enemy.

Standing tents with camp-fires lit in their lines every night were left in position in camps after their occupants had moved on.

A pretended embarkation of troops, within observation of the enemy, was staged at Deir el Belah for the benefit of the Turks. Columns of men belonging to the Egyptian Labour Corps were marched in order down to the beach and conveyed in surf-boats to vessels lying off-shore. Lighted boats were kept moving backwards and forwards till late at night, while next morning trawlers appeared off the coast near the mouth of the Wadi Hesi, some distance north of Gaza, giving the impression that a landing was going to be made in the rear of the Turkish position.

A bombardment of Gaza by the artillery was made on October 27, and on the 29th a naval flotilla of British and French cruisers, destroyers, and monitors continued this from the sea.

Colonel S. F. Newcombe, who had been assisting Colonel Lawrence in Arabia, was in Cairo on sick leave in October, 1917, and while there he proposed that, while

Beersheba was being attacked by the mounted forces, he should distract the attention of the Turks by making a raid on their lines of communication between Beersheba and Hebron. General Allenby gave his consent, and Newcombe selected a party of seventy members of a British Battalion of the Imperial Camel Corps. The party was equipped with ten machine-guns, with Lewis guns and explosives in addition, and with Arab guides set out from Asluj on October 30. Making a wide detour through the hill country, they arrived at Es Semua, twenty miles north-east of Beersheba. From there on the night of the 31st, they moved on to the road leading to Hebron, and cut the Turkish telegraph line. As Newcombe had, previous to the war, been exploring in this district, he was well acquainted with the Arab inhabitants, and he hoped to be able to induce them to help the British against the Turks. In this, however, he was disappointed, so he decided to attempt with his small force to block the road leading north from Beersheba, and so cut off the retreat of the Turks from the latter place. He took up a position at Yutta, covering the road, and dug in there, and effectively blocked the Hebron road for two days. The presence of this small force behind the Turkish front line had a most disturbing effect on Turkish Headquarters in Hebron, and preparations were hastily made for the removal of the staff and material.

The Turks evidently thinking this was the advance party of a larger flanking movement, drew forces from their reserves at Dhaheriya in the north, and from Sheria in the west, thus weakening the centre of their front line at the time when Allenby was ready to drive home the blow that was to make the opening for the mounted divisions to pour through. Newcombe's party was surrounded, but held out till nearly half of the force were killed, and most of the rest were wounded, when

WITH THE CAMELIERS IN PALESTINE

the remainder surrendered. The Turks, meanwhile, had
put up a stout resistance to the advance of the British
force north of Beersheba, and thus prevented the gallant
little company from being rescued.

On the 27th a Turkish reconnaissance in force in-
flicted severe loss on a line of Yeomanry outposts which
had been pushed forward from Karm on the north side
of the Wadi Ghuzzi, two troops being wiped out before
the arrival of the 53rd Division compelled the Turks to
retire.

Two battalions of the 158th Brigade of the 53rd
Division were added to the Imperial Camel Brigade to
form a force called Smith's group under the command
of Brigadier-General Smith of the I.C.C. This force,
including the two N.Z. Companies, left its camping
ground at 8 a.m. on the 30th, crossed the Wadi, and
travelled all day across the flat undulating ground of
No Man's Land till the low hilly country was reached in
the evening. Motor ambulances were met with, carrying
back men wounded in outpost engagements. One Tommy
with a triumphant grin proudly held up a bandaged
thumb; he was wounded, but satisfied.

The I.C.C. dug in after dark on the hillsides, but
during the night moved forward a mile and again dug in.
At daylight on the 31st the infantry on our right could
be seen advancing along the ridges under a hot shell-
fire. The infantry divisions of the 20th Corps met with
determined resistance, losing during this advance 136
men killed and 1,010 wounded.

Our force was dug in at the mouth of a wadi which
opened out on to flat ground leading to the town, the
outskirts of which could be seen from our position. In
the morning a battery of Field Artillery came down the
wadi at a gallop, wheeled into position and in less than
a minute the guns opened fire on the defences of Beersheba; behind us somewhere in the hills, thundered our

heavier guns, and from our position we could see the shells bursting with tremendous effect in the vicinity of the town. Meanwhile the two mounted divisions, the Anzac and the Australian, had travelled some thirty miles during the night from Khalasa and Asluj, and after a very stiff fight the N.Z.M.R. and the A.L.H. had captured the important position of Tel es Saba by the afternoon. At 4.30 p.m. the Fourth A.L.H. Brigade charged, leaped over the trenches between them and Beersheba, and entered the town, when all resistance ceased. About fifteen hundred prisoners were captured by Desert Mounted Corps, with a loss to themselves of fifty-three killed and one hundred and forty-four wounded. The sudden, dramatic charge of the Australians prevented the Turks from damaging all the wells, and the possession of these made Beersheba a watering position as a base for movements farther afield.

Part of the Anzac and Yeomanry Divisions immediately followed the Turks who had retired from positions in the neighbourhood of Beersheba into the hilly country towards the north. Strong opposition was met with by our forces, as the enemy had reinforced their left flank to prevent the next set of wells at Khuweilfeh, some ten miles north, from falling into our hands.

Early in the morning of November 1 the I.C. Brigade moved forward through the defences of the town, where abandoned guns, shells, and here and there bodies of Turkish soldiers, indicated the toll that had been taken the day before by our forces. The camels, the only part of our columns that seemed to fit naturally into the surroundings of mosques and eastern houses, gravely stalked ahead, as their kind had done for thousands of years, through the small town that could trace back its existence to the time of Abraham, and their riders from the far distant lands of the Southern Hemisphere looked with interest on the deserted earthen dwellings and

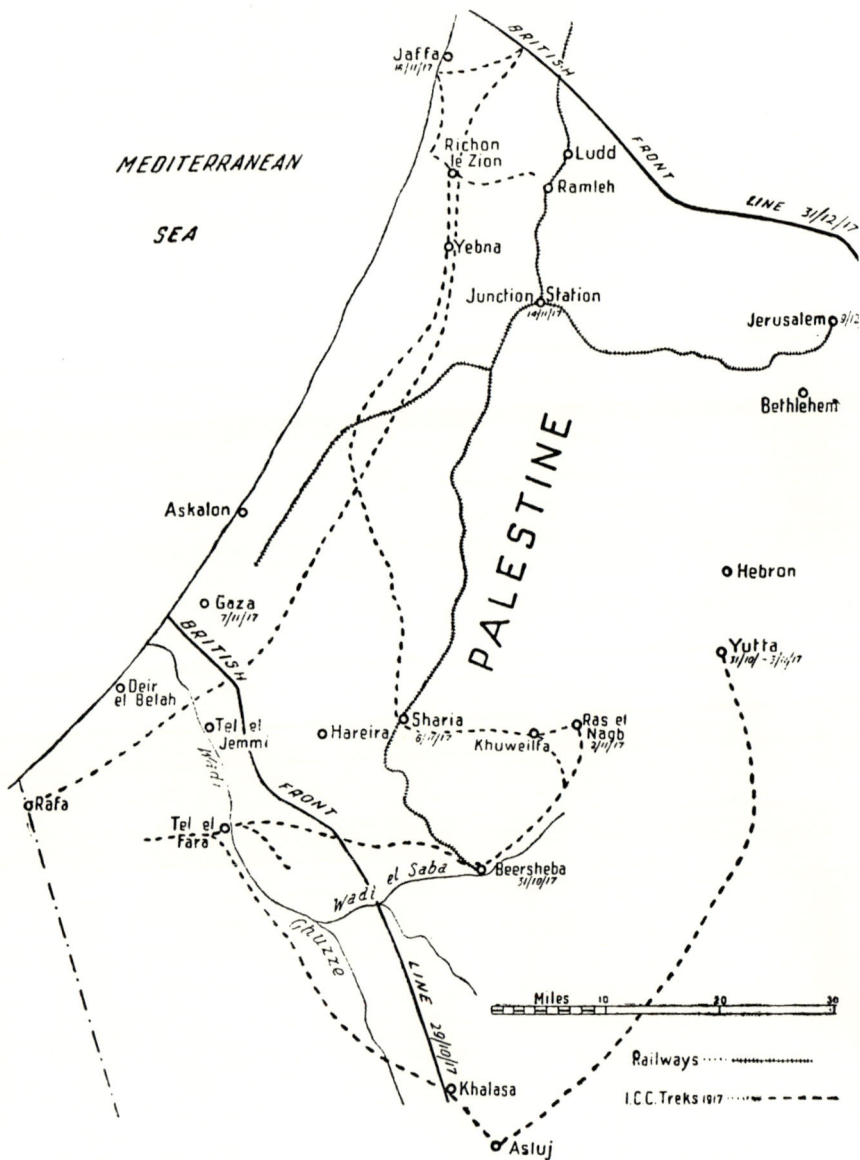

abandoned wells, the latter of which had been the cause of strife ever since Abraham and Isaac first dug them.

The Camel Corps moved on in conjunction with the 53rd Infantry Division into the hilly country north of the town. The transport of the infantry had failed to connect with the Division, and during their advance the Cameliers came across small detached parties of the former searching unsuccessfully for springs or wells at which to slake their thirst. Our men attempted to fill the empty water-bottles, but not being allowed to halt, they spilled more than they supplied from their fantassis.

Part of the I.C.B. were attached to the infantry in an attack on Tel el Khuweilfeh, while the Fourth Battalion relieved the Mounted Brigade on the extreme right of the line. While proceeding to take up this position on the evening of November 5, the Battalion was heading up a wide flat between two ranges of hills, the 16th N.Z. Company leading, when the Intelligence Officer galloped up, wheeled round the head and directed it up a side wadi into the hills. Here the camels were barracked, and left under camel-holders, while the main body advanced up the ridges in the dark in the supposed direction of the front line. The leaders, however, lost their way, and the force sat down in the dark and waited till daylight showed them their position. In the forenoon the camel-holders were ordered to take the animals to the wadi they had been making for the night before, but this time they travelled under different conditions as they were under observation of the Turkish artillery, which immediately opened fire on them, but fortunately the aim was bad, and the only losses sustained were loose articles which fell from the men's baggage, but no one stopped to retrieve these, as the camel-holders, each with not less than three unwilling animals strung out at the full length of neck and halter behind him, were vying

129

with each other as to who could make the quickest passage into the shelter of the wadi for which they were bound. Fortunately there were no casualties, and the camel-lines were formed in Shrapnel Gully before the men of the N.Z. Mounted Rifles filed down it after their relief by the Cameliers in the morning. The camel-holders were able to make some compensation for being behind time by supplying each thirsty horseman with as much fresh water as he could drink.

The Fourth Battalion took over a position along the top of a limestone ridge, including Hill 2023, called Ras el Nagb, which was the key position of our right flank, the New Zealand Companies being on the extreme right of the whole British front line. Just before midnight on November 6, the Turks made a determined attack on the hill, creeping up in the dark and bombing our listening and observation posts. Their superiority in numbers enabled the enemy to gain a footing on the hilltop, but our men, recognizing the importance of our retaining possession of this post, refused to give way, and after a desperate fight, finally drove the Turks off the hill with considerable loss to the latter. From daylight on the 7th, the position was subjected to heavy fire, but all further attempts of the enemy to gain a footing on the hill were frustrated.

On the 8th, the 18th Australian Company attempted to carry out a strong reconnaissance in front of Ras el Nagb, but sustained heavy casualties. All the wounded were not brought in until after dark, and some fine work was done in recovering these, the New Zealanders giving assistance. On the following afternoon the Turks made another attempt to capture the position, and got within a hundred and fifty yards of our post, but the accurate fire of our men and the fine shrapnel practice of the Hong Kong and Singapore Battery beat off what proved to be the last attempt of the enemy to regain the hill.

During one of these attacks a section of the 16th N.Z. Company under a Sergeant held a dominating position of the sector. The force on its left was being pressed so heavily that the Lieutenant in charge there (not a New Zealander) decided to retire his men, and sent a messenger to the Sergeant to retire also. The latter told the messenger to tell his officer to "go to H——, as the New Zealanders will hold their position to the last man." The superior officer yielded to the stronger mind, and the line remained intact. It was not surprising that Sergeant Wilson not long afterwards was sent to an Officers' Training School to obtain his commission.

During the five days that the I.C.C. held this position the camels were watered only once, the nearest water being at Beersheba some fifteen miles away. The camel-holders set off in the late afternoon, and on the way down the wide open valley, one Camelier noticed a bag of durra which had evidently fallen from someone else's saddle. He pulled out of the line with his unwilling string of animals, and barracked them down, being determined to secure an extra allowance of grain for them. As the straps of the bag were broken and the animals were very restive at being left behind, it took some time to fasten the durra on a saddle, and the column was over a mile away when the rattle of machine-guns was heard in its direction. When the rescuer of the durra arrived at the spot where the firing had occurred, he found two of his comrades lying on the ground wounded, waiting for the ambulance from a field-dressing station not far way, while eight camels were lying dead nearby, several others having been wounded. The Turkish planes had raked the column with their machine-guns, and the section where they had struck it most accurately was where the rider had been when he pulled out to salvage the bag of durra. The

Camelier who had moved up into his place in the column had one of his charges killed and another wounded, while the rider behind him received a bullet through his shoulder. "Virtue always brings its own reward," thought the Camelier. "It pays to be thoughtful for the welfare of one's mount."

That night the scene at the wells at Beersheba, when lit up momentarily by the flashes of officers' electric torches, showed nothing but a sea of camels' heads and humps, or the tossing manes of eager horses, held back with difficulty by their holders, who at the same time were vying with each other to reach the water-troughs first in order to let their thirsty mounts be thoroughly satisfied before being moved on by the voice of authority.

At one point at Ras el Nagb one sniper caused us some trouble every time a man moved from shelter. There were no trenches, the only cover being a low line of limestone on the hilltop, and he claimed several victims before a strong pair of field-glasses (not of military issue) detected a movement in a clump of scrub about a thousand yards away. A burst of fire from a Lewis gunner cleaned the spot up effectively. Shortly afterwards a party of Staff Officers rode up the wadi behind us and dismounting, proceeded to a hummock on the sky-line close at hand, where they had a view of the village of Dhahariya ahead, and the road leading north, along which Turkish transport vehicles could be seen moving to the rear. The party drew the artillery fire of the Turks, and a shell flew fairly close over their heads. Every man in the party with the exception of one tall officer ducked; he stood erect like a telegraph pole. Shells still flying, the party retired to where they had left their horses, remounted, and rode away. They had not gone fifty yards round a rocky corner when a shell burst on the very spot where the horses had been standing. The tall officer who disdained to duck was

General Allenby. If the sniper had still been in action, or if the Turks had only known what their target was, and how accurate was their ranging, the Egyptian Expeditionary Force might have had to continue the campaign under a different leader, with what results who can tell. It is good policy to take a strong pair of field-glasses with you to the war.

By the fifth day on which we had been in this part of the line, the pressure of the Turks had been lessened, and the Cameliers were relieved by the Infantry. The Cameliers mounted and moved west past the hill of Khuweilfeh where their comrades of the Third Battalion had, along with the 53rd Division, a desperate but finally successful struggle against the Turks. Of this action General Allenby in his despatches says: " The Turkish losses in this area were very heavy indeed, and the stubborn fighting of the 53rd (Welsh) Division, Imperial Camel Corps, and part of the Mounted troops during November 2 to 6, drew in and exhausted the Turkish reserves, and paved the way for the success of the attack on Sheria."

During the Third Crusade this spot, Khuweilfeh, was the scene of a highly successful raid carried out by Richard the Lion Heart, on June 23, 1192. Richard had word that a very valuable caravan, laden with treasures of all kinds, and stores and arms for the Saracens, was coming from Egypt, so he made a sudden incursion from the coast, and intercepted it here. Mounted on a powerful charger, the King, with lance and sword struck terror into the hearts of his enemies. The description of the fight, as given by a contemporary historian, gives one the impression that Richard mowed down his enemies in the same manner as a reaper in a harvest field, and the harvest was evidently a rich one, consisting of great quantities of gold, silver, spices, valuable garments, arms and coats of mail, etc. If Richard had been taking part

in the fight at Khuweilfeh in November, 1917, he would
have been crouching behind rocks, or crawling on his
hands and knees along hollows on the ground, and his
harvest would have consisted of one substance, under the
circumstances more valuable than all the wealth captured
in 1192, namely, fresh water from the wells.

While these successes were being gained on the right
flank, the 21st Corps on the left of the line had captured
Gaza on November 6, and the 52nd (Lowland) Division
pushed north to prevent the Turks from taking up
another entrenched position. Near Deir Sineid this
Scottish Division met with fierce resistance, and were
driven off a low hill four times, but undismayed they
made a fifth assault, and drove back the enemy in confusion. The attacks on Gaza from November 2 to 7
cost the British just on two thousand seven hundred
casualties in killed, wounded, and missing.

In the centre of the Gaza-Beersheba line, the 20th
Corps drove back the enemy on November 6 and 7,
capturing the strongly entrenched positions of Kau-
wukeh, Rushdi, Hareira, and Tel esh Sheria. Through
the gap thus formed, Desert Mounted Corps poured in
pursuit of the retreating enemy. From the 7th to the
16th the mounted forces kept the Turks fighting rearguard actions, and, by their fierce pursuit, prevented the
enemy from taking up an entrenched position strong
enough to check the pursuing British forces. The broken
nature of the roadless country, the difficulty of obtaining
supplies of water and forage for the horses, and the
ever-increasing distance from railhead, all combined to
form a difficult problem for General Allenby, but the
advance never ceased. From the starting point at Asluj
on October 30 to November 16, the mounted forces
advanced seventy-five miles, and cleared up all the
country of Turks between the Judaean Hills and the
sea as far north as Jaffa.

CHAPTER XV

JAFFA TO JERUSALEM

By the capture of Junction Station, where the main line branched off to Jerusalem, the Turkish force was cut in two, their Seventh Army retiring into the Judaean Hills, where they were followed by the 52nd and 75th Divisions. The Eighth Turkish Army retired along the coastal plain, followed by the mounted forces, past Ramleh, Ludd, and Jaffa (which was captured by the N.Z. Mounted Brigade on November 16), and finally took up a position north of the Auja River.

On November 10 the I.C. Brigade was relieved by the 53rd Division in the hills north of Beersheba, and started on an interesting four days' journey through the land of the ancient Philistines, where they marched across the old front line and up the centre of the coastal plain in the track of the victorious mounted forces. The Cameliers were moved from the extreme right of the British front line at Ras el Nagb to the extreme left on the coast south of Jaffa, and in their journey they saw evidence of the effective work done by Desert Mounted Corps during its sweep north—the exploded ammunition dump at Sheria, transport vehicles with the carcases of horses and oxen still attached, the position at Huj where the Worcester and Warwick Yeomanry made their dramatic charge on Turkish artillery in position, cutting down the gunners with their swords and capturing all the guns.

Leaving Julis at 1 a.m. on November 15, we passed Esdud, the Ashdod of the Philistines and the Azotus of Herodotus, which was a walled city in ancient times. In the year 650 B.C. it was besieged by a Pharaoh of Egypt, Psammetichus I, and of it Herodotus relates: " Psammetichus ruled Egypt for fifty-four years, during twenty-nine of which he pressed the siege of Azotus without intermission, till finally he took the place. . . . Of all the cities we know, none ever stood so long a siege." This record of twenty-nine years for the length of a siege has not been beaten since. A siege of that duration certainly has some advantages for the besiegers, it gets over some of the difficulties of procuring reinforcements. If the soldiers took their wives and families with them, recruits could be reared on the spot.

The Cameliers now passed through more thickly populated country. Small rounded hillocks were scattered here and there over the plain, and on each one was placed a village, Jewish or Bedouin. As they approached Yebna, they came under shell fire, and suffered casualties in men and camels. The first orange groves were met with at Yebna, and these were at once declared out of bounds for all ranks. Next day a limited supply of oranges was distributed by the Quartermaster, but the men had no room for these, as their saddlebags had all been well filled with fruit unofficially the night before. After weeks of bully-beef and biscuits, with no vegetable food, the oranges at Yebna were pronounced by all hands to be the best in the world.

On November 14 the I.C. Brigade was stationed on the sandhills near the sea, in support of the N.Z.M. Rifles who were attacking the Turks on the hill at Ayun Kara, north of Richon le Zion. In his despatches General Allenby states: " On the left the N.Z.M. Rifles had a smart engagement at Ayun Kara (Richon le Zion, six miles south of Jaffa). Here the Turks made a determined counter-attack, and got to within fifteen yards of our line. A bayonet attack drove them back with heavy loss." This action opened the way to Jaffa, which was occupied by the N.Z.M. Rifles on the 16th.

The Camel Corps had meanwhile moved inland towards " Abu Shushe where on the 15th the Yeomanry Division and part of the Imperial Camel Corps had a very satisfactory engagement. The enemy was driven back on Amwas, leaving 400 dead and 360 prisoners, in addition to another ninety captured as the Yeomanry passed near Ramleh in their advance." (Official Record of E.E.F.) The prisoners taken in this big drive were frequently found to be in a very exhausted state, chiefly owing to lack of food and water. One large batch of prisoners under the escort of Cameliers was taken to a well where they nearly went mad in their attempts to get at the water. After being given a drink they lay round the well like animals, rising every now and then to again slake their thirst.

The country round Ramleh and Jaffa appears to be very fertile if properly cultivated. In this area many of the Jewish colonies were placed which were established by the Zionist Movement. The villages were composed of bungalow types of houses, built of wood, and roofed with Marseilles tiles. All were neatly kept, and appeared to be comfortably furnished. The orchards were carefully cultivated, grape-vines, orange and lemon trees being neatly pruned according to modern methods. During the war these Jewish colonists must have led a precarious existence, as they could not export any of their produce, and there was no local market for it.

Near at hand, by way of contrast, could sometimes be seen the Bedouins' attempts at cultivation, where the surface of the soil had been merely scratched up an inch or two deep with their wooden ploughs of the type used in Biblical times, with the result that their barley crops were barely high enough to be cut with a hand sickle.

When camped south of Jaffa, our Company one day had an unusual experience; we were given what was practically a holiday and taken to spend a day on the sea-beach. Leaving camp at 9 a.m., under a sky of cloudless blue, we wound our way between groves of orange trees in full bearing. It was a beautiful sight, the fresh green appearance of the trees spangled with the rich golden globes of fruit, and as we were mounted, we had no difficulty in extracting a contribution from the orchards for the purpose of assuaging our thirst. We rode through the southern outskirts of Jaffa, and reached a beautiful sandy beach, shelving gradually out to sea, in water that was so transparent that every object on the bottom could be distinctly seen for a considerable distance from the shore. Conditions were ideal for sea bathing, and this was enjoyed to the utmost. Yet on this very beach, in the year 1799, four thousand of the Turkish garrison of Jaffa were executed by Napoleon's orders, on the plea that they had broken their promises not to take up arms against the French.

We noticed that the Turks had evidently been prepared to resist a landing from the sea, as trenches had been dug along the top of the low cliffs, but these were not used; the attack came by land, and the town was occupied by the New Zealanders without a fight.

As one of the few seaports on the coast of Palestine and the one nearest to Jerusalem, Jaffa has been concerned in every war in that country from the time when the Pharaohs of Egypt ruled the land. Here, no doubt, were landed the cedars of Lebanon for the building of Solomon's Temple; here were performed some of the extraordinary exploits of Richard the Lion Heart, and here also landed the never-ending procession of pilgrims from the earliest times up to the present.

Jaffa has no proper harbour, only an open roadstead, and cargoes have to be landed in lighters. As soon as it fell into the hands of the British forces supply ships for the army were diverted there at once, and for the next nine months until the next big forward move took place Jaffa was a very busy port.

On November 25 the Fourth Battalion I.C.C. left its quarters near Richon le Zion at 2.30 a.m., and moved across the Plain of Sharon (but no "dewy roses" were apparent) to a position eight miles north-east of Jaffa, known to us as Bald Hill, or Hill 265, where it relieved the Second Battalion. Some Scottish Cameliers whom we relieved told us it was "a good possie," as there was a village a short distance ahead where eggs, milk and .oranges could be bought. One of our patrols did visit the place without noticing anything unusual, but it was found afterwards that an advance party of the Turks must have been concealed there while the patrol was passing through.

At this time the British front line, with its left flank resting on the Mediterranean Sea, swung round in a curve, and then ran south-east across the foothills until it faced east in the higher country, where the 52nd and 75th Divisions were forcing the Turks eastwards towards the Jerusalem-Nablus road. Bald Hill was on an exposed part of the curve facing north-east across low ridges running down to a level plain, two or three miles wide, and extending away to the north. This portion of the front line was held by two Brigades of the Anzac Mounted Division, the 161st Brigade of the Infantry and the Imperial Camel Brigade. There was no continuous line, outposts being placed at suitable positions sometimes not within sight of each other. All troops that could be spared were needed for the more difficult task of forcing the enemy up the gorges and steep ridges leading to the plateau on which Jerusalem was situated.

The day after we entrenched ourselves at Bald Hill, signs of activity could be seen in the enemy's country. Down the level plain between us and the foothills, reinforcements, artillery, and transport vehicles could be seen advancing from the north for the greater part of the day. They would have made a splendid target for our artillery, but we evidently had none in support of us. Our own guns of the Hong Kong and Singapore

Battery were away in support of our forces in the mountain country, so the Turks advanced unmolested. That night was a bright moonlight one and till well on in the morning we were kept awake by a continual howling of jackals in the gullies round about us. Whether it was the moon or the Turks that caused such an outcry we could not tell by further observation as on the following night there was quite a different kind of a disturbance to keep us awake.

When we took over our sector of the line there were no trenches in the position, so we dug in on selected spots on the neighbouring ridges, but dug trenches only long enough to accommodate the small parties into which we were divided. Next morning the Turks began to shell our position. Their guns could be seen across the level flat near the foothills in front of us. At first it was interesting to watch for the flash and then duck down and wait for the arrival of the shell, but a whizz-bang or two soon stopped that practice. The bombardment with shrapnel and high explosives was kept on for several hours, and on our left enemy troops could be seen working their way up towards our line. The attack was so fierce that a company on our left flank was compelled to retire. The Turks entered these trenches and began to enfilade the trench next to it which was occupied by a section of the 16th Company. This section put up a stout resistance, but soon their casualties were so heavy that they were ordered to retire to the next ridge, and to keep the line intact; our other two sections on the extreme right in the afternoon were ordered to fall back also. As we were retiring the Sergeant in charge of our section was wounded and had to be assisted back. He was a general favourite with all ranks, being the leader in all the physical activities of the company. He had a considerable sum of money in his belt, and this was known to the men of his section. One of his comrades, evidently wishing to do something to help his wounded Sergeant, innocently asked if he could carry the latter's money-belt for him. The Sergeant's sense of humour and knowledge of his man refused to see any selfish motive in the offer. During the retirement another member of the section heard that his Sergeant had been wounded, and returned to the trench to see if he could give any assistance, but finding the trench empty, evidently climbed out again to rejoin his party, when he was struck by a bullet, and fell just behind the trench. He was not missed until later on in the day, but his body was found in the evening untouched by the Turks.

We retired to the next ridge and dug in there. So far we had had no artillery or aeroplane support, and at one time five Taubes were hovering round us. Just before dark our artillery came to our assistance and pounded the trenches severely. As dusk fell, the 16th Company counter-attacked the position and charged uphill under a hail of machine-gun and rifle fire. With a yell our men flung themselves on the Turks who fled leaving their machine-gun and all its outfit, with men's kits, some prisoners, and several dead and wounded. To our surprise the only casualty in our party was a wounded finger received by one man. The explanation was that the trench was slightly over the brow of the hill on the Turkish side, and the Turks instead of making use of the trench, had lain down on the front of the low parapet, and so were firing uphill. Our yell must have been well timed, as it had evidently been given just before we appeared on the sky-line, and the Turks, judging by its volume that they were being overwhelmed, fled without waiting to catch sight of us.

The Turks kept up a desultory firing on our position all night and till well on next morning, but their own captured machine-gun helped to keep them at a distance. Two Australian troopers had landed in our trench in the dark along with our section, and shortly after daybreak one of them was struck on the side of the head by an enemy bullet, but did not seem to be badly affected by the wound. He merely put up his hand to the spot, and talked quite rationally about himself while his head was being bound up. When his mate declared that the bullet had passed right through the head the wounded man asked us to look for it, as he would like to keep it as a souvenir. It could not be found, and shortly afterwards he climbed out of the trench, and, refusing assistance, went off with his companion. His sergeant told me next day that the man died that night, and that the bullet had been found embedded in the base of the skull. Wounds, even fatal ones, affected men in many various ways.

On the day of the Turkish attack, the 15th Company's camel lines were heavily shelled, and the camels had to be moved back in a hurry, leaving the men's bivvies and gear behind. The position was under constant fire during the daytime, but one night a party succeeded in recovering all the property safely.

The following days were taken up with artillery duels, and at night raids were made now by one side, now by the other. On the night of December 3, the 17th (Australian) Company made a raid on a trench occupied by the Turks. The small party of about a hundred men moved out after dark to an appointed position to await the signal to attack, which was to be given by a star-shell. Our artillery shelled the trenches heavily, to which the Turks replied in kind. The attacking force lay out on the open hillside, with shells shrieking overhead both ways, and waited for the signal to advance. As they lay there in the dark, anticipating a warm reception, the suspense caused many of the men to take a gloomy view of the prospect, and quite a number asked a padre who accompanied them to take last messages to relatives if they did not survive the night. The padre, who was afterwards awarded a Military Cross for his fine rescue work that night, said later his own heart was in his mouth, and he did not know which way he or the men would run if anyone set a bad example. Suddenly the star-shell burst, and the inevitable wag, who was to be found in every company, recalled all ranks to their proper senses, by calling out in the language of the " ring," so well known to the Aussies, " Gong's gone! Get to your corners, boys!" With a laugh and a cheer the men rushed forward with the bayonet, but the Turks instead of keeping in their trench, were lying out some distance in advance of them, and met the attackers with machine-guns, rifles and bombs, and drove back the raiders with heavy loss, more than a third of them being casualties, three being killed.

The Turks kept searching for our Headquarters and the camel-lines with their artillery, and made our line of communication rather unhealthy. The presence of Bedouins in the vicinity raised a suspicion that they were responsible for the accuracy of the enemy fire. On one occasion a runner from the front line was making his way back to H.Q. when the Turks opened fire on the track. Shells were landing all round him, and he was thrown to the gound by the explosion of an H.E. Looking around he saw near at hand another Camelier lying as flat as he could, and he coolly remarked to him, " Well, Bill, what is it to be, Heaven or Constantinople? Let's give Heaven a go," and he took to his heels and got through untouched.

If the Turks had broken through on this section of the front line, the lines of communication of the British army would have been threatened, and the safety of the Divisions operating in the hills would have been seriously endangered.

On the night of December 4 the Camel Brigade was relieved by the New Zealand Mounted Rifles, and retired to near Ramleh. As the 16th Company was waiting in the reserve trenches for the relief to arrive, the sound of a horse galloping towards them from the rear was heard in the darkness. Down the slope it came, and across the flat, heading straight for the trenches. Some of the Cameliers ran to meet it, and managed to stop it almost on the edge of a trench, and helped the rider to dismount. He seemed almost on the verge of a collapse, and gasped out, " They're coming! There's thousands of them. I saw them back there!" " Who's coming from back there, my lad?" he was asked. " The Turks! There's thousands of them! I saw them!" " Well, they can't come from there, my son. What have you been drinking?" was all the sympathy he got. He was a member of the relief force, and had evidently been sampling some of the wine of the country, and had fallen asleep in the saddle. His horse had wandered off from the column, and when the trooper woke up in the darkness, he mistook his own regiment for what he thought was a Turkish arm, and setting spurs to his horse, he fled, he knew not where.

While the Mounted men were thus engaged, the 52nd and 75th Divisions, and the Yeomanry Division were forcing the Turks back up the mountain sides in spite of the difficulties of the rocky, roadless country and cold wet weather which rendered impassable to camels and limbers what roads had been made. Under these conditions donkeys proved very useful for packing stores, etc. to the troops. By the end of November the 60th and 74th Divisions relieved the 52nd and 75th, and in the beginning of December the 10th (Irish) Division lately arrived from Salonika, took the place of the Yeomanry Mounted Division. The 10th Australian Light Horse was attached to the 60th Division during

144

Brig.-General C. F. Watson,
First British soldier to enter Jerusalem

Reading the Proclamation at Jerusalem, from the Tower of David.   December 11, 1917.

the advance on Jerusalem, and one night they were camped on the historic Field of the Shepherds near Bethlehem. The visit of the Aussies would not have quite the same surprising effect on the minds of the natives as that of the midnight visitors of old, but perhaps the shepherds watched their flocks more carefully that night.

The 53rd Division came north by the Hebron road, and by December 8 the pressure of the British forces compelled the Turks to retire from Jerusalem, which was surrendered on December 9 without a shot being fired in its immediate vicinity.

On December 8 many civilians in Jersualem had received orders from the police to be ready to leave the city at once, but during the day the near approach of the British forces caused a panic to be set up amongst the Turkish troops who retreated, and during the night the whole of the enemy forces abandoned the city, the Governor, Izzet Bey, leaving behind him a letter of surrender. On the morning of December 9 the Mayor of Jerusalem delivered this to Brigadier-General C. F. Watson, who transmitted the information to Major-General Shea, the G.O.C. of the 60th Division, by whom the surrender was accepted. The first intimation of the departure of the Turks was given by civilians to Privates H. E. Church and R. W. J. Andrews of the 2/20th Battalion, London Regiment, while Sergeants Hurcomb and Sedgewick of the 2/19th Battalion were the first to meet the Mayor who was approaching the British position with a flag of truce.

On December 11 General Allenby made his formal entry into Jerusalem through the Bab el Khalil or Jaffa Gate, with an escort which contained representatives of all the forces in his army. A proclamation announcing that order would be maintained in all the hallowed sites of the three great religions, which were to be guarded and preserved for the free use of worshippers, was read in English, French, Arabic, Hebrew, Greek, Russian, and Italian, from the terrace of the entrance to the Citadel below the Tower of David, and thus for the thirty-fourth time in its recorded history of nearly three thousand years the Sacred City of Christendom passed once more into the hands of an invading army.

CHAPTER XVI

RECUPERATION

By the beginning of December 11 the Companies of the I.C. Brigade had fallen considerably below strength. Their casualties had been heavy, and the men in the ranks suffered considerably from septic sores, which broke out whenever a slight injury was received on the skin. Under the strenuous conditions of the campaign proper treatment could not be received; the water supply was insufficient for ordinary health purposes, and was frequently of an impure nature. Infection seemed to affect even the slightest scratch, and often the sores increased in extent to such a degree that the men had to be sent back to hospital for medical treatment. In addition an epidemic of skin disease broke out, and affected most troopers; in one section only one man kept free from the infection. Sometimes the points of irritation turned septic, and men were seen with the whole of both of their arms bandaged on this account.

The camels also were in low condition owing to the strenuous times they had passed through, and most of them developed mange badly, a disease which, if not taken in hand in time, will render the animals useless for service. The weather had become cold and wet, and camels do not stand these conditions as well as horses. The Camel Brigade was therefore ordered back to the dry sandy country at Rafa for medical treatment for men and animals.

The journey south was a most uncomfortable one. Heavy rain began to fall before the Brigade left Yebna and continued to fall on the following days. The whole of the coastal plain became water-logged, the camels, already in a weak condition, sank well over their fetlocks in the soft ground, frequently bogged altogether, and simply lay down and refused to exert themselves further. When a camel gets into this condition it is usually a hopeless task to get it on its legs again. The best thing to do then is to remove its load and shoot the animal to put it out of its misery. One reason for destroying such deserted camels was that they all bore a military brand, and if they fell into the hands of Bedouins it would be difficult for the military authorities to decide whether such animals had been obtained honestly or not by the natives. When all discarded military camels were destroyed, possession of any such branded animal by a Bedouin was sufficient proof that the camel had been stolen.

For five days the Brigade struggled south, its route being marked by straggling Cameliers whose mounts needed careful nursing to keep them going, while every now and then the body of a camel showed that the struggle had been too much for it. At length the Wilderness of Shur was reached, and one night camp was pitched near the redoubt of Hareira, formerly one of the strongest positions in the Turkish line between Gaza and Beersheba. The place was strongly entrenched and heavily wired in, and in front the ridge sloped down gradually to a perfectly level plain stretching seven or eight miles south to the Wadi Ghuzzi. The strong entrenchments on all the ridges and also out in the plain would have made a frontal attack on the position an almost impossible task. Fortunately the outflanking movement at Beersheba and the break through at Sheria compelled the garrison at Hareira to withdraw before their line of retreat was blocked.

The Camel Brigade crossed the Wadi once more near Shellal, but found a country changed from what it had been when last they saw it before Allenby's big drive had begun. Then there were camps and troops everywhere, but now the only signs of life were a few small guards over bridges or watering-plants.

The 16th Company passed one small camp of empty tents under the care of a guard of British Infantry, and when the Company stopped for the night about a mile away one Camelier, whose bivvy shelter of an oil-sheet and a blanket had not proved rainproof on the journey south, set out after dark and returned in an hour or so with enough canvas to make a bivvy that was the envy of the section. He said the guards would not miss it, even if they counted the tents in the morning. He had crept in and cut the inside lining of a double tent without interfering with the guy-ropes, and had left the outside covering of the tent standing. With a little manipulation he was able to shape his new abode so that it bore no resemblance to a tent.

The Brigade halted near Shellal for ten days. Relief parties with led camels were sent back to help the stragglers whose animals had collapsed, and it was some days before all these strays were gathered in. The experience during this trek south showed the state that the camels had got into. An advance into enemy territory under these conditions would have been almost impossible.

While camped at Shellal the Medical Officers prescribed wholesale treatment for the ailments of the men. A supply of a suitable ointment was issued to each company, and each man had his body effectively anointed and massaged by his mate. It was a weird sight to see from the background of night, in the unsteady light of the dancing flames of the bivvy fires, the figures of the men in Nature's garb, ivory white on the side next the fire, and black silhouettes on the other side, rubbing each other's bodies vigorously and indulging in all kinds of pranks and antics like playful schoolboys. It must have looked like a dance of demons, but the accompanying sounds were in no ways demoniacal—there was too much merriment to make that mistake. A fresh issue of warm underclothing was made, and the treatment continued for several evenings. All wearing apparel and blankets were disinfected in a steam chamber; more varied forms of food were supplied (our section got a crate of eggs in one issue, and eggs and bacon appeared on the menu for breakfast for a very short time), and the trouble was soon cured.

The Brigade then moved on to Rafa where the camels were handed over to the Veterinary staff who had a party of Egyptians to carry out the work. The bodies of the animals were treated with a dressing of a very oily nature, washed with hot water and then scraped. They were covered with rugs made of heavy sacking, and as the weather was cold they looked very miserable for some days, but with plenty of food and rest they soon began to recover their condition. Rough grazing was to be had on the sandhills, and after a fortnight's time they were given regular exercise every morning, and gradually hardened up, until by the beginning of March the Brigade was once more ready to take the field.

At the same time means were taken to keep the men fit. Physical exercises were carried out in the early mornings; football matches were arranged in which the 16th N.Z. Company more than held its own against all comers, and occasionally sports meetings were held which consisted of contests for both men and camels.

On December 31 the Third Battalion (including the 15th N.Z. Company which had taken part in the campaign from El Arish to Hill 265) left the Brigade, and moved down to the Canal Zone where it carried out patrols and other duties until the Camel Corps was reorganized in June, 1918. The Hong Kong and Singapore Battery rejoined the Brigade at Rafa on January 5, after taking part in the strenuous hill fighting leading up to the capture of Jerusalem, and on January 16 the First

Battalion (Australian) rejoined the Brigade, having been relieved in the Canal Zone by the Third Battalion. Lieut.-General Chauvel, Commander of Desert Mounted Corps, paid a visit of inspection to the Brigade in January. He addressed all ranks, thanked them for the good work they had done, and afterwards gave an interesting summary of the chief events of the campaign from Beersheba to Jaffa. Lieut.-Colonel Mills, the newly appointed O.C. of the Fourth Battalion, took over his new command early in the year, and at once put himself onside with all ranks.

The hardening process was continued with the camels, and by the beginning of March rumours began to circulate as to what our next move was to be. That it was to be a strenuous one we knew from the insistence of the officers on the necessity of each man having his camel and equipment thoroughly fit, as we were told each man's safety would depend on the staying powers of his mount, and this we found out later on to be quite true. All gear was thoroughly overhauled, saddles were taken to pieces, and the pads restuffed and fitted to suit the backs of the camels, while all leather work was renewed when necessary, oiled, dubbined, and polished.

Early in March the Brigade moved north again. Our Company struck all tents and bivvies, all gear was packed on the backs of camels, and all rubbish was burned, or was supposed to be, and the whole of the sandy area left so level and clean that not a scrap of paper could be seen. Our O.C. viewed the spot with approval, and seemed proud that he had such a conscientious body of men under his command. All hands were in good spirits, everyone was physically fit, the animals were in good form, and we were once more on our road to adventure.

But sometimes appearances are deceptive. After we had trekked some five or six miles, we were overtaken by an irate staff officer who asked our O.C. what the something of a tropical nature he meant by leaving our camping ground in such a disgraceful state, and ordered him to send back a fatigue party at once to clean it up. The O.C. was taken aback, and tried to deny the charge, but higher authority insisted, and the order had to be obeyed. When the fatigue party arrived at our late camping area it found the whole place littered with papers, old clothing, discarded ammunition, bully-beef tins, empty bottles, etc., etc., and looking like a rubbish tip. Apparently as soon as we were out of sight, Bedouins appeared from their places of concealment in the adjoining sandhills, and proceeded to dig in the sand where the bivvies had been, and rooted up the material that the Cameliers had discarded and concealed in the easiest manner possible. Unfortunately the Brigadier and his staff arrived to inspect the site while the natives were so engaged, and our reputation for order and tidiness faded under the hot blast that followed.

The trek north through the centre of the coastal plain was of quite a different nature from our trip south. The country, refreshed by the " former rains," was covered with a thick luxuriant growth of fresh green vegetation, and in the bright sunny days looked like a real Land of Promise. (We were to have an experience of the " latter rains " before long.) Here and there flowers of various kinds grew wild, lilies, irises, cyclamens, stars of Bethlehem, and in places the ground was red with scarlet anemones, all wasting their sweetness in the desert air. For mile after mile no living beings were to be seen, and no signs of habitation or cultivation; the land was as sparsely settled as in the times of the Patriarchs.

In the evenings we would halt on a lonely hillside, and sleep under the stars, reclining amongst the herbage, which gave out a pleasant aroma of wild thyme and other aromatic plants when crushed, and from daybreak the song of the skylark accompanied us in our duties. Occasional swallows were seen, the forerunners of the annual migration to the north, while now and again flocks of ibises were observed. As we moved north villages and Bedouin encampments appeared more frequently, and later on we passed through several villages of repatriated Jews. In one of these, Yasur, the first signs of modern methods of agriculture were apparent, several old drills, a horse hayrake, and an old Deering reaper and binder. These were for many of our lads of more interest at the moment than the ancient eastern implements of the Bedouins.

On March 13, when we were passing through a more thickly populated area, we had halted for breakfast, and just as we were ready to move off two regiments of the New Zealand Mounted Rifles appeared on the march to the east. Men and horses all looked very fit, and many were the greetings from old acquaintances as they passed. At the end of the column medical orderlies and others appeared, mounted on donkeys, but all in the highest spirits. Truly this was a country of contrasts. At one place two Scottish Cameliers were seen chasing a runaway camel, both expressing their opinions of the animal in both pure and impure Doric; a waggon team of five mules is driven past, its driver asking " Can you tell me where be the road to the railway siding, choom?" An Australian Light Horseman rides up to inquire his way to an Aussie Camel Company; a column of British Yeomanry soon appears, and here are New Zealanders mounted on horses, camels and donkeys, while not far off Bedouins are seen scratching the soil with their ancient wooden ploughs drawn by the proverbial ox and ass, or by a camel.

We camped at Ras Deiran for two days, and on the morning of the 17th moved off towards the Judaean Mountains just as heavy rain began to fall. The road soon became running streams of water, or quagmires of mud, through which the camels struggled with difficulty. Two or three collapsed altogether, and one broke its leg in a bog-hole. We followed along the line of the old Turkish railway from Jaffa as far as Junction Station where the column was held up three hours at the crossing of a creek, the bridge over which had been destroyed during the November advance. Leaving the main road leading to Jerusalem, the Brigade turned up a wadi towards the south-east, and wound its way up a rocky road to the higher ground until midnight. Next morning we passed the large village of Zakariyah, set on a hill amidst pleasant surroundings, with olive trees growing freely in its neighbourhood, and then followed a valley half a mile wide, the soil of which was mostly cultivated, which made the going very heavy for the camels. One animal near the head of the column gave up the struggle and was destroyed. Before the middle of the Brigade passed the spot a party of Bedouins had suddenly appeared from nowhere in particular like vultures out of the sky, and had skinned the animal's body, and were wrangling noisily over the division of the flesh. There was going to be a high feast in their encampment that day.

Leaving the valley we followed a rocky track until we reached the top of the plateau some two thousand feet above sea-level. From here an extensive view was obtained of the Judaean Mountains running north and south, while away on the west was the coastal plain, and beyond that the Mediterranean Sea. All day the column passed on over the high country, the only signs of life being seen in the occasional wadis below, where small patches of cultivation formed a marked contrast to the desolate appearance of the rocky sides and tops of the hills around. Towards evening we passed the village of Hausan on our left, when, rising over a bare limestone top, away on the north-east, we caught our first glimpse of the sacred city of Jerusalem, while Bethlehem lay due east of us. The view of these historic spots so intimately connected with the Bible and the three great religions of mankind, had at first a sobering effect on all ranks, not unmixed with which was a feeling of satisfaction that our armies had at length freed these places from the blighting influence of Turkish rule.

From the top of a bare limestone ridge we suddenly looked down on a village, El Khudr, nestling in the valley below us with a fine looking church standing out prominently amongst other stone buildings. This was the Greek church of St. George, which had a clock tower from which the hours and half-hours were chimed. When had we last seen a church or heard chimes? Spanning the road from El Khudr is a well-built stone archway surmounted by an iron figure of the Saint, and having a carving on the arch itself of the scene depicting the slaying of the dragon by St. George, formerly familiar to us on our English sovereigns.

The Brigade camped for three days on a flat piece of ground about a mile below Bethlehem. On one afternoon leave was granted to half of our Battalion to visit the town. The Church of the Nativity was naturally the centre of greatest interest. A flight of steps leads down from the main body of the church to the Chapel of the Nativity in which a silver star bearing the Latin inscription " *Jesus Christus natus est hic de Virgine Maria,*" is inlaid in a recess to mark the supposed site of the birth of Christ. A number of lamps are kept burning constantly in this recess, under the watchful care of the attendants. While one party was being shown through this part the guide remarked of a certain lamp that it had been burning continuously for five hundred years, whereupon an Australian in the party retorted, " Well, it is time the blinking lamp had a spell," and blew it out. A New Zealand Sergeant was speaking to a British Officer in the church when the ancient priest in charge of the vault approached them, and with tears streaming down his face, informed them of what had occurred. The matter was reported to the Officer in charge of the town, and the whole church was placed out of bounds for the troops during the rest of their stay in the neighbourhood. The offender was severely dealt with by the military authorities, but if such an incident had happened in a Moslem mosque, the offender would have been lucky had he escaped from the building alive. Happily there were few instances of thoughtless conduct of this nature amongst the troops.

Some three or four miles south along the road to Hebron, are three large reservoirs, called Solomon's Pools, which once supplied Jerusalem with water. These are 120 yards, 140 yards, and 215 yards long respectively, and vary from 75 yards to 90 yards wide, their depth being from thirty to forty feet. The walls have a smooth cement surface, so hard that it cannot be scratched with the blade of a knife.

Leaving Bethlehem one evening the Brigade passed on towards Jerusalem. The column moved slowly along the Jaffa Road on the western side of the town, past the Bab el Khalil, or Jaffa Gate through which General Allenby had made his triumphal entry on foot, past the high stone walls of the old city, through a well-formed but rather narrow street in the newer part of the town outside the walls, where the Hotel Fast was lit up by electric lights, a sign of modern progress, while in the centre of the old city in the dim moonlight rose the dome of the Church of the Holy Sepulchre, and on the opposite side of the town in the Temple area could be seen the top of the Dome of the Rock, or Mosque of Omar.

As the Brigade slowly wound its way round the northern side of the city, where there was an unobstructed view of the massive stone walls with their arched gateways, such as the Bab el Amud, or Damascus Gate, one could not help dwelling on the tragic history of Jerusalem in the past when time after time it had been captured and sacked, more than once being completely destroyed, while now in these modern times of powerful artillery and high explosives, it had fallen into the hands of the British without a shot being fired over it, or a stone in its walls being disturbed.

The column passed down and crossed the Valley of Kedron, with the Garden of Gethsemane and the Mount of Olives on our left, and slowly climbing the slope of the hills overlooking the Sacred City from the east, it travelled on past Bethany, and at daylight arrived on the hill-tops at Talat ed Dumm. This spot commands a view of the Jordan Valley and the mountain country beyond it, and is a short distance from the Good Samaritan's Inn beside the Jerusalem-Jericho Road. But what a difference in the traffic from that in the time of the Parable. On that day when the man fell among thieves, we read of only three other travellers on the road, and one of them came only by chance, whereas on this day of March, 1918, there was almost a continuous procession of motor lorries, motor cars, limbers, waggons, and columns of transport camels, travelling both ways both by day and by night.

The next day the Brigade camels were taken down to the Wadi Kelt to be watered. The track led down the side of a very steep rocky gorge, and was so narrow that two camels could not pass on it. Each man had four animals, the head of one being tied to the tail of the one in front of it, and in this way the long column wound its way for hours down the narrow track worn out of the steep sides of the gorge. At one point an extra large Bikanir camel could not pass under an over-hanging rock, neither could it turn to go back, so it was pushed bodily over the edge of the track to take its chances of landing alive at the bottom of the gorge.

Just where a tributary wadi joined the main one, an ancient aqueduct about eighty feet high spanned the bed of the stream. It had a wide high arched opening through which the track passed, and must have been an ambitious project when it was built. It was up this gorge of the Wadi Kelt that the Children of Israel, under their leader Joshua, passed when they invaded the hill country of Canaan after they had captured Jericho. Now the cosmopolitan Camel Brigade was retracing the tracks of the Israelites in the opposite direction. We were bound for Jericho, the Jordan River, and the Mountains of Moab.

CHAPTER XVII

THE RAID ON AMMAN

DURING the latter part of December, and in the month of January, the Turks had been pushed north across the River Auja on the north of Jaffa, and in the hilly country north of Jerusalem the infantry kept forcing the enemy back in spite of the determined resistance of the Turks and the rough and broken nature of the country. The weather was frequently cold and wet, which added to the discomforts of the troops and to the difficulties of transport. By the middle of February seven of our infantry divisions held the front line which ran in a south-easterly direction from a point on the Mediterranean coast ten miles north of Jaffa, across the coastal plain and the mountains of Judaea to the high country overlooking the Jordan Valley and the Dead Sea. The Anzac Mounted Division captured Jericho on February 21, drove the Turks north past the Wadi el Auja, and cleared the lower part of the valley as far as the River Jordan.

In March General Allenby decided to make a raid on the Hedjaz railway on the high land east of the Jordan River. A special force was formed under the command of Major-General Shea, General Officer Commanding the 60th Division, and was known as Shea's Group. This force consisted of the Anzac Mounted Division, the 60th Infantry Division, and the Imperial Camel Brigade, along with a heavy and a mountain battery of artillery, and two bridging trains.

One reason for the raid was to draw off Turkish forces from positions farther south where the Arabs were operating against them. Another reason was to attempt to destroy a railway tunnel and viaduct at Amman so as to interrupt the lines of Turkish communication with their base.

159

Amman, the point aimed at, is some thirty miles east from Jericho, and is situated on a plateau 3,500 feet above sea-level. There were no bridges over the Jordan River, and there was only one formed road east of it, leading to Es Salt, but even this was out of repair, the other routes being mere tracks quite unfit for wheeled transport, especially during wet weather.

At 1.20 a.m. on March 22 an officer and nine other ranks of the 2/19th Battalion, London Regiment of the 60th Division swam over the Jordan unobserved at Makhadet Hajla, and prepared the way for rafts to cross, and by 8.10 a.m. the first pontoon bridge was finished under a severe fire from the Turks who had excellent cover from the jungle of tamarisks fringing the river's edge, and also from the higher terrace over-looking the stream from the eastern side. The engineers of the Desert Mounted Corps Bridging Train deserve great credit for the splendid work done by them in bridging the Jordan which was in high flood at the time.

Early on the morning of the 23rd the Auckland (N.Z.) Mounted Rifles crossed the Hajla bridge, and galloped down detachments of Turks in prepared posts with machine-guns in position, thus clearing the way for the engineers to throw another bridge across the river higher up at Ghoraniyeh, and the Anzac Mounted Division and the 60th Division crossed later by these.

At 7.30 p.m. on March 23 the I.C. Brigade left its camping ground on the bare Judaean hills at Talat ed Dumm, and marching all night made its way down the steep mountain road, through Jericho, and across the Jordan Valley to within half a mile of the northern shore of the Dead Sea.

The reality of crossing the Jordan was a marked contrast to the dreams of childhood's days. On a sway-ing pontoon bridge built in less than eight hours mostly in the dark, and exposed to rifle fire, the Cameliers made

I.C.C. crossing Jordan River

Road to Amman

Arabs near Amman

Ten days without wash, Jordan Valley

THE RAID ON AMMAN

their way over the swollen discoloured river, urging on
an unwilling camel in front, and leading a more unwilling
one behind, their view cut off on all sides by the tall
tamarisks on both sides of the river, with the bodies of
casualties, both British and Turks, lying still unburied
on the banks, while the sound of artillery and machine-
gun fire ahead showed that the enemy were still not
far away.

The Cameliers moved up to the foothills near the
mouth of the Wadi Kefrein, and halted there in the
afternoon. This side of the Jordan Valley appeared to be
better watered than the western side, and running streams
of water delighted the eye, and provided the necessary
material for a refreshing wash up for all hands.

A party of Bedouins who were camped near at hand
appeared to be a finer built and more independent type
than any we had hitherto seen. They, no doubt, were
responsible for the stripping of the dead bodies of Turks
we had seen on our way from the river, not an article
of clothing being left on them. The men were tall, erect
in bearing, and each one carried a rifle slung over his
shoulder. Their tents were composed of black material
woven out of goats' or camels' hair, one piece being
nearly forty feet long.

At 6 p.m. the Cameliers mounted and rode on up the
wadi. As they entered the hills, rain began to fall, and
soon the track became very slippery. About 10 p.m.
the column was halted, and from ahead came the rumbling of wheels. In the darkness we could see battery
after battery of artillery making their way to the rear;
the country was too difficult for them to negotiate, so
the column moved on without them. We missed their
assistance later on very materially. The small nine
pounder mountain guns of the Hong Kong and Singapore Battery mounted on the backs of pack-camels,
however, kept with us.

As our point of departure from the Jordan River was little above the level of the Dead Sea, which occupies the deepest depression on the earth's surface, being 1,292 feet below sea-level, and as our objective, the top of the tableland of Gilead and Moab is over 3,000 feet above sea-level, our animals with their soft padded soles had to climb over 4,000 feet up steep rocky mountain sides where the goat tracks were soon converted into quagmires with the passage of so many animals over them, an undertaking camels were never intended for, but their riders compelled them to do it.

During the whole of that first night after leaving the plain, the Camel Brigade struggled up the rough track in darkness, rain and mud. The long night seemed as if it would never pass, but at length daylight broke, and we found we were evidently on the top of a plateau, but mist and clouds surrounded us, and the rain kept falling steadily so that no view of the surrounding country could be obtained. Just after dawn broke at one point the sound of dull blows could be heard at the bottom of a steep slope. Peering down in the dim light we could see a camel wedged in the narrow rocky creek bed at the bottom. The animal had fallen from the track down the steep hillside, and was unable to rise again, and as we were in enemy territory the tall Australian Veterinary Sergeant, not daring to use his revolver lest the report should be heard by any Turkish patrols in the vicinity, was attempting to destroy it with his bayonet.

Still the column moved on slowly with frequent halts owing to animals falling and blocking the track. In the afternoon we came up with an Australian Light Horse Regiment whose transport had failed to connect with it, and it was without food for both men and horses. Each Camelier handed over two days' supply of rations and grain to the Light Horsemen, and carried on with a sufficient supply for themselves. The Horsemen acknowledged that the Cameliers had the advantage over them in the commissariat department at any rate. Night fell once more, but still the Brigade moved on, each man watching keenly ahead, not for an enemy, but for a sight of the tail of the animal ahead of him, as if he lost sight of that beacon he would most likely wander off into the darkness, to be recorded later in the list of "missing." The inclination to go to sleep was almost overpowering, but sleep was not yet our portion. Shortly after midnight we were aware that we were passing through a village, which turned out to be Naaur, and still we went on, camels slipping and having to be helped up again, and still on and on in the darkness and the everlasting mud and rain. At daybreak the rain ceased, and the country being more open, the going was easier. A halt was made about midday, and after a hasty meal, all who were not told off for duties, turned in and slept till well on into next morning, having had a period of eighty hours' strenuous travelling since their last slumber.

Sir H. S. Gullett, in his Official History of the Australian Light Horse, writes: "The ascent of the Light Horsemen, however, was an easy task compared with the terrible climb of the Camel Brigade. Immediately after leaving the foothills, General Smith was obliged to dismount his force, and all night the men of the three Battalions dragged their camels up the mountain-side. The men hauled and urged, the camels slipped and fell, but still fought steadily on. The Brigade straggled in single file almost from the valley to the Plateau, winding its fantastic course along crooked and flooded wadi beds, and treading narrow ledges round the sides of the hills. In peace time such a feat would have been deemed impossible by any Eastern master of caravanning; but under the brutal lash of war the Brigade went surely up to the tableland. 'The camels were carried up by the men,' said Smith next day. No less fine was the performance of the Egyptian drivers with the pack-camels which carried supplies and explosives."

All this was merely preparatory towards the demolition of a portion of the Hedjaz railway south of Amman, which was the duty for which the Fourth Battalion was told off, while the First and Second Battalions took part in the general attack on Amman itself.

The Fourth Battalion blew up some five miles of the Turkish railway between Libben and Kissir stations, as described elsewhere (Chapter XII), and then moved north to Rujim Taihin where it joined up with the right flank of the New Zealand Mounted Rifles in its attack on the Turkish position.

While the mounted forces were struggling up the mountain tracks, the 60th Infantry Division moved up the Wadi Shaib to the town of Es Salt, the largest town east of the Jordan, from which the Turks retired as the British advanced. Leaving a Brigade in Es Salt, two Brigades of the 60th Division advanced towards Amman, fifteen miles to the south-east. The Second Australian Light Horse Brigade attacked on the left of the line, the 60th Division being on their right, the First and Second Battalions of the Camel Brigade were next in order, with the New Zealand Mounted Rifles on their right, while the Fourth Battalion I.C.C., including the N.Z. 16th Company, later on joined up on the extreme right flank of the line.

The Turks were well provided with artillery, and as they had railway communication with their rear, reinforcements were hurried down to Amman. One party of Austrians was captured by us the morning after it arrived in the front line, and the members of it seemed very much disgusted at their fate. The only artillery on the British side were a few light mountain guns and these soon ran out of ammunition.

On the right flank the Fourth Battalion I.C.C. and the N.Z.M. Rifles were subjected to attack after attack on the 28th and 29th, but all these were repulsed, and the line was gradually advanced in the direction of Hill 3039, which overlooked the town of Amman. At 1.30 a.m. on the 30th an advance on Hill 3039 was made, led by the Auckland Mounted Rifles and the Fourth Battalion I.C.C., over a flat tableland for a distance of half a mile, where the Turks were driven out of their position at the point of the bayonet. The Canterbury and Wellington Regiments then advanced through this position and captured a second line where they were joined by the Cameliers. Another advance carried them to the crest of the hill overlooking Amman where protection had to be built up with whatever stones and rocks could be procured, as the covering of soil on the limestone ridge was so shallow that trenches could not be dug. All day long this exposed line was subjected to an intense fire from artillery and machine-guns, and counter-attack after counter-attack was made by the Turks, but each one was gallantly repulsed. The 16th N.Z. Company occupied a forward position on the northern slope, but being exposed to a deadly fire, it was withdrawn to the extreme right flank. During one of these determined attacks to recapture the hill-top the Turks advanced almost to the muzzles of the rifles of our men who, gallantly led by their officers, swept them back down the slope once more. Lieutenant Crawford of the 16th Company moved out openly to direct his men and was struck down to die later on from his wounds, Lieutenant Thorby of the same Company led charge after charge until he fell mortally wounded, as also did Lieutenant Adolph. In the heat of one attack Corporal MacMillan of the Lewis Gun Section of the Company was seen advancing and firing his gun from his hip, until he too fell. Trooper McConnell, one of the regular pack-men of the Company, had gone up to the line with reinforcements. He had a supply of bombs in his charge, and when the Turks counter-attacked almost to our line, he ran forward to meet them, and continued pulling out the pins and throwing the bombs with deadly effect right into the ranks of the enemy, until he fell pierced with bullets. The same spirit animated the whole Company, and the enemy was held off till darkness fell.

The Second A.L.H. Brigade, the Infantry Division, and the other Battalions of the I.C.C. were also held up on the left and in the centre of the front line, and as Turkish reinforcements were being hurried across the Jordan towards Es Salt, and from the north to Amman, it was evident that without strong artillery support the capture of the town would entail heavier casualties than would be justified by the gain, and so a retirement to the Jordan Valley was ordered.

Great difficulty was experienced in evacuating the wounded. The casualties were heavy, the dressing-station was a mile and a half behind the front line, the way to it was over a flat table-top exposed to both shell and machine-gun fire, and stretcher-bearers were frequently hit while attempting to cross it.

On the morning on which the advance on Hill 3039 took place, the N.Z. Brigade Medical Officer, a New Zealand Colonel, and the Fourth Battalion M.O., a New Zealand Captain, agreed to work together, and they examined the wadi to find the most suitable spot for a dressing-station. The Captain went towards the head of the wadi, but seeing no sheltered spot he returned to meet the Colonel, who reported that farther down there was a cave that would be an ideal place, but that they could not get the use of it as an Australian M.O., evidently a Colonel, had possession of it and said it was going to be used by the Camel Corps, and the New Zealanders could go elsewhere. " But I am the only Camel Corps M.O. with our Battalion. .I wonder who this Colonel can be," said the Captain. " Well," replied the New Zealand M.O., " He had not a tunic on, but I think he must be a Colonel by his high-handed manner, and judging by his language I am certain he is an Australian." " I had better go and see him," said the Captain. " Perhaps we can arrange matters suitably." When they arrived at the cave, the " Colonel " was standing at the entrance, and proved to be the Captain's own dresser, one of the characters of the Company, an old soldier with a smart soldierly appearance whose silk shirt, neat strides and putties, as well as his authoritative style of speech had evidently carried full weight with the New Zealand colonel. Tom was merely looking after the interests of his own party. When the wounded cases began to arrive this man worked day and night assisting the Doctor. On the third day while provisions were being forwarded to the front line, two large stone jars of hot Bovril were dropped at the dressing-station, and Tom was urged to take a drink as he looked completely worn out. " No, d—— it," he replied, " I won't touch it. Give it to the wounded. They need it more than I do." The spirit of Sir Philip Sidney still exists. After the retirement from Amman this man was so run down that he was ordered into hospital by his Doctor to recuperate before rejoining his unit.

From this dressing-station to the nearest clearing-station the serious cases who could neither walk nor ride, had to be carried ten miles in camel cacolets or tied on the backs of horses. The tracks were so rough and slippery that time after time the animals fell, causing intense agony to the sufferers on their backs. One example will show what the wounded men had to endure on this journey. A camel cacolet consisted of an arrangement of two stretchers, hung one on each side of a special saddle, in which the patients lay. Two men had always to be carried, the weight of one balancing that of the other, on the opposite side. One Camelier Sergeant had been wounded in the arm, and in spite of his protests, he was ordered back by the M.O. who had to threaten him with arrest if he disobeyed his orders. He had to occupy a place in a cacolet to balance the weight of an Australian Light Horseman who was badly wounded in both legs, and who was quite incapable of helping himself. An Egyptian led the camel, and every time the animal stumbled the Australian fluently called down imprecations on the heads of both camel and leader. Several times the side of the cacolet caught on projecting rocks, and the Light Horseman was thrown to the ground, and had to be lifted back on his stretcher by the Egyptian and the wounded Sergeant. During the whole journey the patient never let a groan or murmur about his own suffering pass his lips. Perhaps he found more relief the other way.

This method of evacuating the wounded was an agonizing experience to them, but it was the only available means of saving their lives or preventing them from falling into the hands of the Turks. From the clearing-station the wounded were conveyed to the Jordan Valley in limbers, another ten miles, and from there motor ambulances carried them to the railway, some seventy miles from the front line. All cases that could be safely moved were then forwarded in hospital trains to Cairo, a further journey of over two hundred miles, the total journey from the front sometimes occupying a fortnight or more.

The retirement of the whole of Shea's Force from Amman took place on the night of March 30. When the wounded had all been cleared from the dressing-stations, the various units retired, some by way of the

Es Salt road, and some through the village of Ain es Sir. The Fourth Battalion I.C.C. made its way in the darkness over muddy roads and down a narrow rocky gorge, and arrived at Ain es Sir at daylight. As it passed through the narrow streets of the town down into the Wadi Sir, one could tell by the looks of the Circassian inhabitants that they were no well-wishers of the British cause. At the bottom of the steep sides of the wadi a fair-sized stream had to be forded, and the passage of so many animals across it made the crossing almost impossible for the camels which slipped continually on the wet slippery banks, but at length the ford was passed. The track then ascended the steep hillside leading to the top of a ridge from which an extensive view was obtained of the table-land extending to the south, and also of the Dead Sea, the lower Jordan Valley, and beyond these the bare hills of Judaea. One Camelier wondered if we were passing over the hill from which Moses had obtained a view of the Promised Land before he died, and on being told it was on one of the hills that we could see that this event occurred, he quite solemnly remarked, " Well, I don't wonder that the old geezer turned up his toes rather than go into that God-forsaken country! "

The day of our return to the valley was a day of bright sunshine, and the flowers on the hillsides, refreshed by the recent rains that had caused us so much discomfort, were blooming freely, and made this countryside a marked contrast to the bare hills on the western side of the Jordan. But many a rider saw little of the beauty or the view, as worn out by the strenuous experiences night after night in the front line, followed by a long night's ride during the retirement, many Cameliers fell asleep on their saddles, only to waken up momentarily when their mounts stopped to graze, or when roused by their comrades to keep the column intact.

The N.Z. Mounted Brigade acted as rearguard to the retirement by the Wadi Sir, and when the last squadron of the Wellington M.R. was passing through Ain es Sir, it was fired on by the inhabitants and by a body of Turks who had followed in pursuit, and eighteen members of the squadron were either killed or wounded.

During the raid the British captured nearly a thousand Turks, but had 215 of their own force killed and 1,010 wounded, while 123 were posted as missing.

In the list of honours granted for services performed in these operations the 16th Company I.C.C. was well represented. Military Crosses were awarded to Lieutenants R. F. Mackenzie, A. G. R. Crawford (died of wounds), V. E. Adolph (died of wounds). Sergeant A. G. Hooper and Trooper R. Maxwell (died of wounds) were awarded the decoration of D.C.M., and Trooper T. Parker was awarded the Military Medal, while Sergeants H. S. Jones and M. Kirkpatrick, and Lance-Corporal L. Pask were mentioned in despatches.

CHAPTER XVIII

A BIBLICAL PARALLEL

WHAT a story the town of Amman could tell if it was able to relate the whole of its history from the time that the Children of Israel under the leadership of Moses captured it along with Og, the king of Bashan, the last of the giants, the size of whose bedstead excited the amazement of Moses so much, as is stated in the Book of Deuteronomy. In Old Testament times the city was called Rabbath Ammon, and later on, about the year 300 B.C. it was rebuilt by Ptolemy II of Egypt (Philadelphus) and named Philadelphia in his honour. It was later an important stronghold of the Romans, and signs of their occupation are still seen in the Citadel and the well-preserved remains of the amphitheatre which was capable of seating four thousand spectators.

The country in the neighbourhood of Amman is not desert, but consists mostly of a fertile limestone tableland capable of growing wheat of first class quality. It must have once been thickly populated, judging by the numbers slain in the wars waged here by King David and other kings of the Israelites.

During one of these campaigns there occurred an incident most discreditable to David, when, to obtain possession of a beautiful woman whom he coveted, and who afterwards became the mother of Solomon, he designedly sent an honourable soldier to his death.

Having become enamoured of Bathsheba, the wife of Uriah the Hittite, David, from his palace in Jerusalem, sent a message to Joab, the general commanding his army which was besieging Amman, to give leave to Uriah, to return home to report to him on the state of the war. One can imagine Uriah making his way over the high tableland, "on leave," until he overlooked the

Jordan Valley, and saw in the distance the mountains of Judaea where lived his wife in the city of Jerusalem. When he arrived at the capital, he reported to the king who then gave him a portion of his own viands, and bade him enjoy leave for a day or two at home. But instead of going home, Uriah " slept at the door of the King's house with the servants." When David heard this next day he sent for Uriah, and asked why he had not gone to his own home. Uriah replied, " The ark, and Israel, and Judah abide in tents, and my lord Joab and the servants of my lord are encamped in the open fields; shall I then go into mine house to eat and to drink, and to lie with my wife? As thou livest, and as thy soul liveth I will not do this thing." David then set meat and drink before the soldier, who partook of these luxuries so freely that he became drunk, but still he refused to go home.

Foiled in his attempts to prevent his own immoral relations with Bathsheba from being discovered, the king decided that Uriah must die, but in such a manner that he himself would not be blamed for the soldier's death. He wrote a letter to Joab, telling the latter that Uriah had offended him, and he commanded the general, " Set ye Uriah in the forefront of the hottest battle, and retire ye from him that he may be smitten and die."

Uriah was directed to return to the army and was given the letter to be delivered to Joab, and he once more crossed the Jordan, and climbed the mountain side to Amman, little dreaming that he was carrying back his own sentence of death. Joab carried out David's orders, and praising Uriah for his bravery, sent him with a storm troop to break down part of the wall of the town. The garrison made a sally, Uriah's companions, acting under instruction, retreated, but he himself, as Josephus records, " Ashamed to run away and leave his post, sustained the enemy, and receiving the violence of their onset, he slew many of them, but being encompassed round, and caught in the midst of them, he was slain."

And now in March, 1918, British, Australian and New Zealand troops were attacking the same town where Uriah fell some 2,950 years before, and strange to relate, the incident of carrying a letter to a commander, and of being left " in the forefront of the hottest battle " was re-enacted in the experience of a New Zealand Camelier on the night of the retirement of the British forces from Amman.

In the afternoon transport camels had arrived at the camel lines with supplies, and a trooper was despatched with two sacks of provisions, two fantassis of hot tea, containing five gallons each, and a stretcher, to take them if possible to the front line. On the way in he met the Colonel of the Fourth Battalion I.C.C., who gave him a written message to deliver to the officer in charge of the Cameliers at the front. He had to cross an open tableland about a mile wide, which was being swept with Turkish shells and machine-gun fire, so half way across, the camel being too good a target, was barracked in the shelter of some rocks. The trooper made a copy of the Colonel's message (and so unlike Uriah, knew the contents of the letter he was carrying) and gave it to his companion to take in later if he himself was unable to deliver the original. The message contained instructions regarding the manner of retirement after dark, and was safely delivered by the trooper, who then returned for the camel and its load, which was safely brought up behind the line under the cover of darkness. The trooper worked his way along the line in the dark with the supply of hot tea, which made him as popular as Kipling's Gunga Din with the troops, as their water bottles had long been emptied. A trooper standing at his post near a gap in the limestone escarpment was offered a drink, but he declined, saying, " Give it to that poor devil of a Turk down there." Some distance below him lay a wounded Turk, moaning in the darkness for "Moiyi! Moiyi!" (water, water). But there was sufficient for both the modern Sir Philip Sidney, the second example met with on the same day, and the wounded Turk as well.

Replacing the fantassi on the camel which he had tethered to a clump of scrub in a sheltered spot, the Camelier made his way to his own Lewis gun section of four men on the extreme right flank of the front line. Firing still continued along the line, but in the darkness figures could be seen moving to the rear. As time went on, no orders arrived for the small section, and no further movement was observed. After a little while, knowing that a retirement had been decided on, the Camelier who had brought in the message, offered to go along the hill to see what was taking place. He made his way cautiously from cover to cover in the darkness, but could find no trace of any troops except the piles of empty cartridge shells where earlier in the night he had seen machine-guns. Rifle shots still rang out in the darkness, but from what direction he could not tell. Not knowing whom he might encounter, he cautiously made his way to the highest point of the ridge, when his guarded hail was answered by a voice challenging him, "Who goes there?" He replied, "A friend," and advanced to find Captain M. Johnson of the Auckland M. Rifles who was covering the retirement with his troop, and was keeping up a desultory fire to lead the Turks to believe that the line was still occupied, but who was just on the point of withdrawing his men. The Captain advised the Camelier to tell his section to retire immediately or they would be left to the tender mercies of the Turks. On his way back to his companions, and he did not waste any time on the way, the Camelier thought if the Turks decided to advance on the position, that the British army was rather poorly represented in numbers (but not in quality) in that sector. When Captain Johnson went back to his post he found that his lieutenant had already withdrawn the men, but a sergeant was waiting impatiently for the Captain lest he should lose touch with his troop. It seems to be a fairly common custom at Amman for individual soldiers to be left " in the forefront of the hottest battle," but in the case of the Cameliers this was not intentional as it was in the case of Uriah, as three out of the four officers of the 16th Company had been killed or mortally wounded during the day, so it was not to be wondered at that one small group should be overlooked in the dark.

The Camelier rejoined his section, and led them to where the camel was barracked. A small quantity of tea still remained in the fantassi, and this quenched the thirst of the small party. The Lewis gun with its drums and boxes of ammunition, a spare rifle or two picked up, a spare overcoat containing a wristlet watch and some coins in the pocket, were packed on the saddle, and the section retired with all the honours of war, and safely made its way across the tableland to the camel-lines. It evidently pays to know the contents of letters you carry to Commanders at Amman. Poor Uriah's education must have been neglected, or he lacked the initiative given by a training in a Colonial Camel Corps.

CHAPTER XIX

At midday on Monday, April 1, the Fourth Battalion I.C.C. left its camping ground amongst the thorny thickets of scrub at the mouth of the Wadi Shaib in the foothills on the east side of the Jordan, and moved down the sloping plain towards the river. All that forenoon, Christian and Jewish refugees from Es Salt, a town situated in the mountains of Gilead, 2,000 feet above sea-level and twenty miles from the Jordan River, poured down the road past the camp in an unbroken stream—men, women, and children, some well dressed, many evidently of the poorer class, all carrying whatever they could of their worldly possessions, in bundles in their hands, or on their shoulders; little children in their mothers' arms, or carried on the backs of their older brothers or sisters; all fleeing from the treatment they knew would be meted out to them when the Turks regained possession of Es Salt on the retirement of the British forces. One could notice the feeling of confidence they had in British protection, when, some miles from the river, they were met by our limbers and waggons, and when the women and children were loaded into these, they sank down contentedly on the bottom of the vehicles, worn out but satisfied that they were in safety. At the Ghoraniyeh Bridge over the Jordan all weapons were taken from the men, and a rare collection of arms of all kinds, ancient and modern, was gathered into heaps by the roadside. The refugees were given a meal of bully-beef and biscuits, and were taken later on to suitable camps in various parts of the country until after the armistice.

We crossed the plain on the west side of the river, and camped that night close to the historic town of

Jericho (native name Eriha), which is situated 1,100 feet below sea-level, and is the lowest situated city on the face of the earth. Immediately behind us was a flat-topped hill called Jebel Kuruntal, or the Mount of Temptation.

As were were standing by in the morning, a trooper asked his mate what the hill was, and he was told that Kuruntal was the native form of the Latin word *quadraginta,* meaning " forty," and that Christ, after fasting for forty days, was there tempted by the Devil to worship him, the latter offering Him all the country He could see if He did so. The trooper whose biblical knowledge was rather vague, asked if the offer was accepted, and on being told that it was not, remarked in all sincerity, " I'm d——d if I would have done it myself if the country was the same then as it is now." We had, during the last ten days, made a fairly thorough survey of the wilderness round Jericho and it certainly possessed few attractions for a New Zealand farmer.

The known history of Jericho extends as far back as the time of the invasion by the Children of Israel some 3,300 years ago. In those days it was a walled city, which, built near the mouth of a gorge leading directly to the plateau of the Canaanites, commanded the most direct route from the east to the Promised Land, and it was necessary that the Israelites should capture it so as to give them access to the higher country. This was accomplished with a musical accompaniment in the dramatic manner described in the Book of Joshua.

Jericho must have been a much more prosperous place in those olden times that it was when captured by our mounted forces in February, 1918, as in the former times it had a king and government of its own, and it evidently was a place of some wealth, judging by the booty taken by one individual in the army of the Israelites, and retained by him in spite of the strict orders of

Joshua to the contrary. This man, Achan, appears to have secured a fair amount of loot, as, when accused by Joshua, he confessed, " When I saw among the spoils a goodly Babylonish garment, and two hundred shekels of silver, and a wedge of gold of fifty shekels weight, I coveted them and took them, and behold they are hid in the earth in the midst of my tent."

In our case we were not warring against the inhabitants of the cities, but against their oppressors, the Turks, and so the property of the residents was respected. But history repeats itself; 3,300 years after Achan's time, our Company, on its way to carry out a reconnaissance on our flank, camped at nightfall near an army dump where there was a supply of poles for telephone lines. We were out of firewood, and had not the wherewithal to boil up, and in less than ten minutes after we had halted, there was a procession of telephone poles moving into our lines. There was only one axe in the outfit, and it worked overtime that night. Next morning, leaving the bulk of our equipment in our lines under the guard of two men, we moved off to our allotted task. Not a sign of a stick was to be seen, either on our saddles, or amongst our baggage, or along our lines, for " behold they were hid in the earth in the midst of our tents," but when we returned at night, a stab with a bayonet in the sand under each bivvy brought to light a supply of firewood. We were more successful in using this method of concealing our booty than Achan was, but in our case we had not plundered private individuals, and we had not received specific instructions that we were not to use telephone poles for firewood. The ordinary Camelier, under such circumstances, did not feel he was committing a crime; he was merely keeping himself fit for further active service in the face of an enemy (which is a good soldier's first duty) by judiciously transferring the use of an article (in this

178

case, telephone poles) from one arm of His Majesty's service (the Engineers), to that of another (the I.C.C.).

In any case there was little temptation to indulge in looting in modern Jericho, as the houses were poor hovels, and the inhabitants, a few hundred in number, were a sorry looking lot. The Wadi Kelt, a narrow ravine with precipitous sides, issues from the Judaean Mountains at Jericho, and provides a permanent supply of water to the town, but the country showed almost no signs of cultivation, and the vegetation was mostly thorns. Most of the pests connected with the plagues of Egypt at the time of the Exodus of the Israelites were to be found in the valley. Ashes and dust as of old, produced boils and blains wherever the skin was broken; flies, fleas, lice, and mosquitoes (of the deadly malaria-carrying type) made air raids or night attacks with deadly persistence, while spiders, snakes, and scorpions appeared to be well dug in under stones, etc., and one never knew when he would experience a surprise attack from these pests. Jericho is the only village in the deepest depression on the land surface of the globe, with a hot, humid, unhealthy atmosphere, and is the nearest inhabited place to the centre of the earth. The troops who were there during the summer of 1918 now understand exactly what is meant when they are told to " Go to Jericho."

Yet in the time of the Romans, Jericho was a prosperous city, situated in the midst of large groves of date-palms, plantations of bananas, and cornfields, and was celebrated for the spices produced there. Mark Antony made a present of the city to the fair Cleopatra, who afterwards sold it to Herod the Great. It became a place of residence of the latter, and he died here about the year 4 B.C. Remains of old stone walls, dumb witnesses of its former prosperity, are still standing in the vicinity.

On the evening of the day after our crossing the Jordan River, our force pushed on some twelve miles up the Jordan Valley to relieve some British infantry in the front line. It was rumoured that it was to be for only forty-eight hours—it turned out to be forty days before we were relieved. We did not exactly fast for forty days in the Wilderness, but it could not be said that we lived on the fat of the land—if so, it was a very lean land.

The Camel Brigade occupied the front line from the foot of the Judaean Range on its left flank, to the west bank of the Jordan River on its right, a distance of some six or seven miles. The slopes of the mountains on the left were so steep and so cut into by impassable gorges, that they did not require to be held by either force. From the foot of the slopes with the exception of an outstanding hill or two, the ground sloped gradually down towards the river, in places overgrown with thorny scrub, in other places perfectly bare, and crossed at intervals by dry beds of vanished streams, some narrow, some broadening out into wider wadis with bulrushes growing in their lower portions, but all with steep banks, so that there were few crossing-places in them, except where the wadis ran out up on the plain, or where they joined a larger channel near the river itself. The First Battalion occupied the left of our line, with its left flank resting on the steep eastern slopes of the mountains. Included in its sector was a prominent steep-sided hill called Musallabeh, jutting out on the plain, and dominating the whole of the flat country adjacent to it, and also commanding the approaches to several fords in the lower Jordan Valley. The right of the front line was held by the Fourth Battalion, with its right flank held by the 16th N.Z. Company, resting on the west bank of the river. At first the Company held outposts in advance of the Wadi Auja, the only one containing a running stream of water, but later they advanced to the Mellaha Wadi, two miles farther forward. Observation posts with Lewis guns in each were manned in the day time, and the presence of some of our Scottish friends from the Machine-gun Squadron with their guns gave us a feeling of confidence. At night parties went out on outpost on exposed parts of the plain, dug trenches, and erected barbed wire protection.

Our artillery, including some six inch guns, were placed in the Wadi Auja in our rear, and there opened out on the enemy positions at fairly regular intervals, observers usually coming up to the front line to observe the results, and direct the fire. As all hands became used to this routine, things became rather casual. Once, instead of sending an observer forward to our post, the artillery officer rang up the latter, and said our guns were going to open up on a Turkish redoubt ahead of us, and asked the occupant of the outpost to record the result. Bang went the gun. " About a mile and a half to the right," was the report. " But we want the correction in yards," came back over the wire. " Well, multiply the blinking number by 1,760, and you'll get it for yourself," was the reply as the telephone rang off. After that we were not asked again to act as deputy forward observation officers.

The living conditions were very unpleasant in these wadis, the sides and floors of which were quite devoid of vegetation of any sort, and day after day the rays of the burning sun poured down unmercifully. Lieut.-Colonel Preston in his book, *The Desert Mounted Corps,* states: " The average maximum daily temperature during July, as taken at the R.A. Headquarters on the top of the Tel el Sultan-Abu Tellul Ridge, was 113.2 degrees Fahrenheit in the shade. The highest reading recorded during the month was 122 degrees and the lowest, 107. At the foot of the ridge the temperature was about three degrees higher, and at Ghoraniyeh it reached 130 degrees on several occasions. During August the temperature rose still higher, but no daily record was then kept of the thermometer readings. The tremendous evaporation from the Dead Sea keeps the atmosphere moist, and adds to the discomfort caused by the great heat, while the increased air pressure, due to the depth of the valley floor below sea-level, induces a feeling of lassitude against which it is difficult to fight."

The only shelter one could get from the sun by day was by propping up an overcoat or blanket, and crawling underneath it, but the small flies which were present in clouds also watched the erection of these shelters and immediately swarmed into them, and gave the occupant no peace. At night as the flies settled down the mosquitoes became active, the adjacent swamps being natural breeding grounds for these pests. One could not leave any part of one's body exposed, or the mosquitoes discovered it, and so, muffled up over the head in a blanket in the close humid atmosphere, one was soon bathed in perspiration, so that sleep at night was far from restful. The Turks did not believe that white troops could exist in the valley through the summer of 1918, and a Turkish aeroplane dropped a note behind our lines to say that they would come along and bury our bodies when we were dead. It is very interesting to receive an assurance while you are still alive, that your funeral will be well attended, and our men were so interested that they decided that they would wait and see the ceremony themselves, but as it happened, it was the Turks that had to be buried.

As all supplies for the forces in this district, two Mounted and one Infantry Divisions, and the Imperial Camel Brigade, with numerous extras, had to be transported by road from the nearest railhead some forty or fifty miles away, and then distributed by limbers or pack camels to the various units, it was not surprising that everything except bare necessities were a minus quantity, but although rations were simple in the extreme, we were never without something for a meal. Even our mails were delivered to us in the front line with as much regularity as we could expect. It was wonderful how both letters and parcels found us, no matter in what directions we or they had been wandering, as evidently the mail bags had their adventures also. One trooper received two parcels which had been posted on the same day in December, 1917, at a country post office in New Zealand, and on April 16, 1918, both parcels were delivered to him in the wadi Auja, but one had stamped on it, in addition to the address which was still quite legible, the words, " Salved from torpedoed ship." The parcels had evidently been despatched by different vessels, one of which had been sunk by the enemy, but the mails had been afterwards salvaged, the contents of course of this parcel being spoilt. Little things like this let us know that war was being carried on below sea-level elsewhere than in the Jordan Valley.

During the month of April, 1918, General Allenby's army suffered a severe loss by the transferring of the 52nd and 74th Divisions, nine Yeomanry regiments, ten British battalions of infantry, five and a half siege batteries, and five machine-gun companies for service in France, while in May fourteen more battalions of British infantry were also withdrawn for the same purpose. Their places were partly supplied by Indian forces, which in many cases had not seen active service, and were therefore of less value than the hard-fighting experienced forces they replaced.

Some of these Indian companies were attached to the I.C.C. in the Jordan Valley during the hot months of 1918, but the men did not seem very happy, as they were unable to carry out many of their usual customs.

For one thing the scarcity of water was irksome to them, as they were unable in their spare time to indulge in the practice of washing their long hair and winding it carefully round their heads, with a turban encircling the whole. On one occasion the writer was able to shake a party of these Indians out of their phlegmatic state, and get a cheerful smiling response from them, but what was the reason he did not fully realize at the time. Early in 1917, when the 16th Company I.C.C. was returning from a week's raiding in Turkish territory in the south of Palestine, the writer had to go with a group of four Cameliers to relieve, just as darkness fell, an outpost of Patialla troops who were helping to guard our lines of communication. The Subadar in charge was a cheerful, hefty Indian who could speak English fairly well. He was in high spirits at being relieved, and as he was leaving us he said in farewell, " Sut, sree akal." On being asked what that meant he replied, " All the same as good-bye, good luck." " All right then," I replied, " Sut sree akal to you." " You no English, you say that. You Indian," he said. " All right, Sut sree akal." I retorted, as he disappeared in the darkness, but the phrase remained in my memory.

Some months later, when returning from a class of instruction at Zeitoun, I had to wait for the night train up the line at Kantara where the Suez Canal is crossed. While wandering about the large military camp there in search of cigarettes of which there seemed to be a shortage in the canteens, I came to the area set apart for the Indian troops. Seeing a canteen open, and hearing voices within, I entered, but immediately the voices stopped, their owners who were sitting on the sand playing some native game, became like Buddhist idols, and the attendant behind the counter assumed the expression of the Sphinx. I sensed opposition immediately, and felt that any business transaction was out of the question, but an inspiration came. " Sut sree akal," I remarked blandly. Instantly the Sphinx became an animated being, and the idols came to life. " Sut sree akal," was responded on all sides. " Have you any cigarettes, Johnny? " I asked. " Yes, plenty," was the ready reply, and the deal being completed to the satisfaction of all, I retired with honours, to the accompaniment of " Sut sree akal."

In April, 1918, when a party of Indians attached to the I.C.C. in the Jordan Valley was moodily proceeding up the Wadi Mellaha on its way to outpost duty, it had to pass immediately in front of the writer's bivvy. " Sut sree akal," he remarked, when instantly all faces turned towards him with expressions of pleasure in every feature, and a united response of the same refrain, " Sut sree akal." After that he seemed to be the most popular white trooper in the Wadi with these Indians, but why, he knew not.

Years afterwards when he was settled down once more in civil life in his native land, the writer read in a New Zealand daily paper a cable from India which stated that a tribe on the North-west frontier, called the Akali, had raided a town in the lower country, had looted the bazaars, and had marched in force through the main streets, firing their rifles, and shouting their war-cry, " Sut sree akal." Evidently the cry was the password of an unfriendly society on the border of India, and the writer had been passing this on as if he was one of the initiated, and he had evidently been accepted as a member without further test. A little knowledge is sometimes a dangerous thing, but in this case he had if anything the better of the deal.

But life in the valley was not allowed to pass along in this uneventful manner. The Turks had their programme to keep us busy, and the British had plans also to stir up the Turks, and both of these affected us.

During the night of April 10, a sudden burst of enemy fire was heard across the river and farther down its course, and in the early morning the Turks advanced against the British positions guarding the bridgeheads on the eastern side of the river. The Infantry and the Australian Light Horse held up this attack, and the enemy had to retire. At the same time a determined attack by the Turks was made on Musallabeh, the hill on the left of our front line. Artillery, machine-guns, bombs and rifle fire were brought to bear on the position held by the First Battalion I.C.C. (Australian), but the men hung grimly to the post. All day long the attack was hotly pressed with heavy casualties on both sides. The Turks tried to outflank the position, and got so near that they were able to throw bombs into the lines of the Cameliers. The latter responded in the same manner, and with the arrival of reinforcements of men and munitions were able to drive off the enemy. *Military Operations,* the Official History of the War, states: " At Musallabeh the Turks were only prevented from taking that invaluable hill by the coolness and steadiness of the Camel Corps."

Trooper Bluegum sums the result of this fight as follows:

"Oh! Allenby came smiling o'er the hills of Palestine,
    And victory came hot upon his track.
He sent congratulations to the Camels—said 'twas fine;
    Said he knew that we could keep the blighters back.
And to celebrate the battle, lest the world forget the deed,
    And the day we gave the foeman such a bump,
'Now and henceforth and for ever,' he solemnly decreed,
    'Musallabeh should be called The Camel's Hump.'"

On April 29 the 16th Company I.C.C. advanced from the Mellaha Wadi for a distance of a mile, and took up a position with one half company on its right flank on the high terrace immediately overlooking the Umm esh Shert ford over the Jordan, the other half company occupying a position on the tableland about half a mile to its left, the space between consisting of dry wadis with almost perpendicular sides of soft crumbling bluish-gray clay, up which it was quite impossible to climb. The party on the right were in the front seats in the dress circle for the next act that was just going to be staged, and before they were withdrawn were to attract the attention of some of the actors at some cost to themselves.

The road from the Umm esh Shert ford led directly across the flat ground which rises gradually to the foot of the Mountains of Gilead to a leading ridge up which lay the direct road to the town of Es Salt, some ten miles away. This level piece of ground immediately across the river from us, and directly under our observation, was to be the scene of a fight on the result of which depended the safety of a large part of Desert Mounted Corps. If the Turks were successful General Allenby might not have had at his disposal the whole of the efficient cavalry force which finally swept the Turks out of Palestine and Syria in September and October, 1918.

The Turkish army held a strong position at Shunet Nimrin in the range of hills lying east and parallel to the Jordan River northward from the Dead Sea. The lines of communication to its base and the railway at Amman, consisted of two roads, one a partly metalled road passing up the Wadi Shaib through the town of Es Salt, and thence over the tableland to Amman, the southern and unformed one passing through Ain es Sir, lay open to attack from the adjoining territory of the Beni Sakhr tribe of Arabs. If the Desert Mounted Corps could force its way up the east side of the Jordan and up the mountain road to Es Salt, and gain a commanding position in the rear of the Turkish Infantry, one line of communication of the Turks would be cut, while if the Arabs blocked the Ain es Sir road there was a chance of capturing the whole Turkish force so strongly entrenched at Shunet Nimrin.

In his despatch describing the British operations east of the Jordan, General Allenby states that a deputation from the Beni Sakhr tribe waited on him, saying that the tribe was concentrated near Madeba, within striking distance of the Turks, and was ready to co-operate with him if an advance was made at an early date. Everything seemed to promise success in the undertaking, if only promises could be relied on, especially Arabs' promises.

On the night of April 29 our artillery bombarded the enemy's trenches at Shunet Nimrin, and the infantry attacked this position at the same time. This attack was continued day and night till May 4. On the same night the mounted forces crossed the Jordan at Ghoraniyeh and moved up the valley as far as Umm esh Shert, where the Fourth Light Horse Brigade pushed on as far as Jisr ed Damie, some fifteen miles from Ghoraniyeh, while the main force turned at right angles to the valley, moved up the mountain road to Es Salt, and seized the road beyond it to Amman.

Colonel Lawrence, in his *Seven Pillars of Wisdom*, tells that at this time he visited General Allenby's camp, and learned to his amazement that some chiefs of the Beni Sakhr had offered the immediate co-operation of twenty thousand tribesmen at Themed. Lawrence knew that there were not four hundred men, and at the moment there was not a tent at Themed, as the tribe had moved south. The expected help from the Arabs came to naught, and the Turkish line of communication through Ain es Sir remained open for reinforcements and supplies to be hurried in to Shunet Nimrin.

Meanwhile up the Jordan Valley misfortune had befallen the Fourth Brigade. It had been unable to reach the bridge at Jisr ed Damie, owing to strong machine-gun fire, and Turkish reinforcements of cavalry and infantry crossed the bridge to the eastern side of the river, and forced the Brigade to retire into the foothills. The teams of two batteries of artillery attached to it were shot down, and the guns had to be abandoned, along with limbers, waggons, ambulance and water carts. The retirement of the Brigade through the hills was of an extremely difficult and dangerous nature, owing to the broken and precipitous country traversed. At one spot four camels loaded with fantassis of water, toppled backwards owing to the steepness of the hill they were attempting to scale, and fell three hundred feet to the bottom and were killed. Wounded troopers were rescued by their comrades with difficulty, and it was only by the coolness and bravery of the troops that the Brigade was saved from being cut off altogether. The position of the four Mounted Brigades in the mountains, the First, Second, and Third A.L. Horse, and the Fifth Mounted Brigades, now became serious, and two regiments of the N.Z. Mounted Rifles and a regiment of the Sixth Mounted Brigade were placed under the command of Major-General Chaytor, and hurried up the valley to keep open the line of the retirement of the forces from Es Salt.

Major-General Hodgson, who was in command of these Brigades, received orders to retire, and early on the morning of May 4 the town was evacuated. The Turks made a determined effort to break through the defending forces, but Chaytor's defence held. On the opposite side of the river from their high terrace overlooking this position, the New Zealand Cameliers saw the artillery duel being waged continuously for forty-eight hours, and at daylight on May 4 saw the head of the long column of mounted troops winding its way down the leading ridge directly opposite us, and in full view of the Turks, who began to land shells amongst the leading troops who were spread out in open order, but the route was soon altered to dead ground, and the column moved down the valley in safety. It was one of the few occasions during our campaign when a whole mounted division could be seen in full view on the move under fire.

By midnight that night the artillery duel had ceased, and when day broke on the 5th there was not a sign of our troops on the other side of the river, but the Turks could be seen feeling their way down the valley. They worked their way as if on parade, and took no risks of surprises. Gradually they approached the river opposite us, and seemed surprised when we let them know we were still there. It was quite interesting to watch through a strong field glass, the drill movements of our enemy, especially as we knew it was only a matter of hours when their attention would be transferred to ourselves. As daylight broke next morning increased numbers could be seen in the position in front of us, and as the ground was very broken and gave good cover they soon worked forward to a ridge about five hundred yards away. Our observation post occupied the crest of a prominent projection overlooking the ford, and soon it was the target of a rapid and very accurate fire. Spraying the top of the opposing ridge with a Lewis gun made the enemy keep within cover, but as there was scrub and low trees growing along the banks of the river, the position was rather awkward as if the Turks reached this cover they could have worked their way unobserved to our rear, and cut off our retreat. While this point was receiving attention from our Lewis gun, voices were heard in our rear, and a troop of Yeomanry appeared to relieve us. The other half of our Company on the left meanwhile had beaten back an attack by the Turks, but at a heavier cost in casualties than we had.

That night we retired to the reserve line, not knowing at the time that this fight was to be the last we would take part in as members of the Camel Brigade, as it had already been decided by the C.-in-C. that as the camels had outrun their sphere of usefulness, and as horses would be more effective in the campaign ahead, the Camel Brigade was to be reorganized into a cavalry force.

The Es Salt raid had great possibilities. If the scheme of the British had been carried out as planned, the greater part of the Turkish Fourth Army might have been captured, which would have affected materially the future campaign of General Allenby. Whereas if the attempt of the Turks to break through opposite the Umm esh Shert ford had been successful, five British Mounted Brigades might have been cut off, which would have given an equal advantage to the other side. No territorial advantage was gained by either army. The British casualties in killed and wounded amounted to 1,512, while 137 were posted as missing. Most of these losses were incurred by the infantry in their frontal attacks on Shunet Nimrin. The Turks must have suffered fairly heavily, and in addition lost 942 of all ranks as prisoners, while twenty-nine machine-guns were also captured by the British.

A mistake on the part of the Turks on May 1 prevented them from gaining the full advantage of their position. The Turkish Second Regiment had marched to Mafid Jozele, between Umm esh Shert and Jisr ed Damie, and had crossed the Jordan by a pontoon bridge there when its commanding officer received an order that his force should cross at Jisr ed Damie. This officer evidently believed in literally obeying orders, so he led his regiment back across the river, marched five miles up the stream to ed Damie, and then crossed again according to his instructions. If this regiment had advanced direct from Mafid Jozele and strengthened the attack on the Fourth A.L.H. Brigade before reinforcements for the latter arrived, it would have made matters much more serious for the Light Horsemen.

On May 12 the Camel Brigade left the Jordan Valley, and travelling by night, retired to its former camping-ground on the hills at Talat ed Dum. Leaving there at dark the following night, it followed the road past Bethany and Jerusalem. In the grey light of the early morning our column wound its way down the slopes of the Mount of Olives, past the Garden of Gethsemane, and up the western side of the Kedron Valley, and on past the massive north wall of the ancient City of David, but we did not halt; the exigencies of war do not make provision for sight-seeing; that had to come later on. By 6 a.m. we arrived at a pleasant-looking village called Enab on the Jerusalem-Jaffa road, and there camped amongst its olive groves. Water and firewood were plentiful, and after a real wash and a good breakfast, all hands turned in and slept till well on in the afternoon. At nightfall we saddled up, and once more followed the main road down the gorge leading to the coastal plain, where we made our way to our old camp site at Ras Deran.

The campaign had now progressed past the country which was suitable for camels to operate in. The next military movements were planned to take place mostly in hilly territory where there was a better supply of water than had been available formerly, so it was decided to reorganize the Camel Brigade into a cavalry force. The ten Australian Companies were formed into the 14th and 15th Regiments, forming a new Brigade, the Fifth Australian Light Horse Brigade, under the command of Brig.-General G. Macarthur-Onslow, to which was attached a French Cavalry Regiment, while the 15th and 16th N.Z. Companies of the I.C.C. were formed into the Second N.Z. Machine-gun Squadron, under the command of Major D. E. Batchelor, and attached to the same brigade.

And so in June, 1918, the Australian and New Zealand Cameliers said good-bye to their camels which had carried them in comfort over desert and wilderness, and had even attempted to carry them up the sides of mountains, and once more the troopers returned to horses. They left behind them many advantages in the shape of extra comforts and equipment, which the camels could carry, but the restoration of their spurs gave them a sense of dignity they had missed as Cameliers. By their efforts in the campaign from 1916 to 1918 the troopers had won their spurs as deservedly as many knights-errant of old.

The six British Companies of the I.C.C. were retained for some time, and two of them were despatched in July to co-operate with the Arabs under Colonel Lawrence, in a raid on the Hedjaz railway in the vicinity of Amman.

But the camels themselves, although set free from the service of their former riders, did not yet get their discharge from the war. Colonel Lawrence, in *Seven Pillars of Wisdom,* describes how he obtained the use of them for his Arab forces. He was on a visit to General Allenby at the latter's camp in May, and he relates: " At tea-time, Allenby mentioned the Imperial Camel Corps in Sinai, regretting that in the new stringency he must abolish it and use its men as mounted reinforcements. I asked, ' What are you going to do with the camels? ' He laughed, and said, ' Ask ' Q.' '

" Obediently, I went across the dusty garden, broke in upon the Quartermaster-General, Sir Walter Campbell—very Scotch—and repeated my question. He answered firmly that they were earmarked as divisional transport for the second of the new Indian divisions. I explained that I wanted two thousand of them. His first reply was irrelevant; his second conveyed that I might go on wanting. I argued, but he seemed unable to see my side at all.

"I returned to Allenby and said aloud, before his party, that there were for disposal two thousand two hundred riding camels, and thirteen hundred baggage camels. All were provisionally allotted to transport, but of course riding camels were riding camels. The staff whistled, and looked wise, as though they, too, doubted whether riding camels could carry baggage. A technicality, even a sham one, might be helpful. Every British officer understood animals, as a point of honour. So I was not astonished when Sir Walter Campbell was asked to dine with the Commander-in-Chief that night.

"We sat on the right hand and on the left, and with the soup Allenby began to talk about camels. Sir Walter broke out that the providential dispersing of the Camel Brigade brought the transport of the —th Division up to strength; a godsend, for the Orient had been vainly ransacked for camels. He over acted. Allenby looked at me with a twinkle. 'And what do you want them for?' I replied hotly, 'To put a thousand men into Deraa any day you please.' He smiled and shook his head at Sir Walter Campbell, saying sadly, 'Q, you lose.' It was an immense, a regal gift, the gift of unlimited mobility. The Arabs could now win their war when and where they liked."

CHAPTER XX

CAMELIERS AT PLAY

BUT war in the East was not always a serious matter, and the Cameliers seized whatever opportunities they could to indulge their sporting propensities. When in reserve in the wilderness the men in the ranks of the I.C.C. had to make their own amusements for their leisure time.

On the evening of the day on which the 16th New Zealand Company arrived at the Training Depot at Abbassia, its introduction to the 15th N.Z. Company took the form of a contest to decide which should have the honour of representing New Zealand in a tug-of-war at a garrison sports meeting which was to be held in Cairo a few days afterwards. The 16th Company won, and later on justified its selection by winning, without a single defeat, the competition at the sports meeting in which eighty-four teams competed.

Boxing contests were frequently held, and in Rugby football the New Zealanders, both in the Camel Brigade and in the Mounted Rifle Brigade, made quite a reputation for themselves.

Sports meetings were occasionally organized, and there was always keen competition between the various battalions represented. Trotting races and scurries for camels produced some " dark horses." Bookmakers freely followed their profession at these gatherings, but did not amass fortunes, as the financial standing of most Cameliers did not allow heavy plunging.

Wrestling bareback on camels produced some unexpected results, as those taking part never knew what their mounts would do. A camel never got excited, but in the middle of a contest would calmly begin to stalk off on its own, carrying its protesting rider with it, or would walk away from under its owner while the latter was held in the grip of his opponent, as he vainly attempted to stop the camel by holding on to its bare hump, which was about as effective as trying to stop a liner from leaving a wharf by holding on to it with one's hands.

A competition in " musical chairs " was mostly a matter of luck, as if there was not a " chair " (a bag of sand) at the spot where a camel was when the music stopped, it was almost impossible to pull him along to where there was one. Camels object to being hurried unless the persuasion is applied from behind.

An egg and spoon race on camels was certainly an innovation in sports in the wilderness, and created quite as much interest for the spectators as the more serious events. To see the big hefty Sikh, Rur Singh, with solemn face, concentrating on balancing an egg in a spoon at arm's length, while urging his big Bikanir camel to increase its pace, and at the same time to keep on its course, was a sight never seen before on a sports ground. The camel was the only one on the ground that did not laugh at the result.

The big brawny Sikhs of the Hong Kong and Singapore Battery, our Bing Boys, were good sports, and held their own in such events as running and jumping, but a hop-step-and-jump contest was too complicated for them, as the tremendous initial hop they made always gave them such an impetus that they could not control the succeeding step, and so were always disqualified, but they laughed with the rest of us at their failures, and made up for it by defeating the 16th Company at a straight-out tug-of-war, the only team in the Brigade that did so. Their gun-mounting competitions were very interesting, and their handling of the guns from the time they took the parts from the backs of the camels until they had them mounted for action excited the admiration of all. 196

Usually the sports day ended up with a concert. A concert party would be provided by some of the Home divisions, and sometimes first-class talent, both male and " female," was procured. There was no door charge, the stage was made of sand-bags and sand, all seats were free and on the same level, on the ground, except for a few chairs or boxes in the " orchestral stalls " for the Heads and their guests, perhaps the back seats in the " pit " were occupied by mounted men from neighbouring units, who with the darkness of night as a background, sat on horseback, while overhead the stars in the sky looked down serenely on the " stars " on the stage. Sometimes a *prima donna* was introduced, whose coquettish manner and falsetto voice always scored a success, or perhaps a female (?) of uncertain years, and garments of a Victorian age, who would protest that although she might be a " has-been " she objected to be called a " Was-ir."

At ordinary times less strenuous amusements were indulged in in the evenings. The members of the British Companies patronized the game of " Housey," which was evidently considered a legal one according to King's Regulations. It was amusing to hear the man who ran the " House," calling out the numbers as he drew them out of a bag. " Legs eleven " (11), " Kelly's eye " (1), " Two little dooks " (22), " Blind fohty " (40), "Clickety click"(66), "Top o' the 'ouse"(90), etc.

The tastes of the Australians and New Zealanders ran more to " Two up " and " Crown and Anchor," but these games were not allowed to be carried on within the lines, so in the dusk, the " schools " assembled out in the sandy wastes where the faint light of their few candles could not be seen from the camp. Especially after a pay day, the " schools " would boom at night, when various schemes were adopted by the rival " ring-masters " to attract custom. Some would have free biscuits and lemonade distributed amongst their patrons at intervals during the evening; others would have a free issue of cigarettes and chewing gum, while their exhortations to the motley crew who were in various states of dress and undress, and composed of men from the four corners of the earth, urged their patrons to stake their piastres on their fancy in a manner that would have turned an American sideshowman green with envy—" Shower it in thick and heavy," they urged, " You pick 'em and I'll pay 'em," " I'll hide 'em and you find 'em," " Throw it in my lucky lads, they come here in wheelbarrows and go away in motor cars." " Speculate and accumulate," " Pour it in, lads. We are the Good Samaritans you read about." " Here's where you get the oscar for your next trip to Cairo."

Egyptian or Sudanese labourers were sometimes employed to carry out the drudgery work of the camps behind the lines. Once a newly arrived Egyptian asked an older hand why the men went out amongst the sandhills at dusk every night. The other replied, " The New Zealanders are very religious men. Their priests lead them out to a quiet spot where they can pray. The priest spreads out a holy mat with marks on it which means something they have great faith in. He kneels down beside the mat, then a row of worshippers kneel all round him, with another row bending over them, and another row standing behind them. The worshippers throw their offerings on to the holy mat, and the priest places two coins on a short piece of polished wood which he calls a Kip, and raising his eyes to the sky, he throws up the coins as an offering to Allah. All the worshippers raise their eyes also to the sky, and then bow solemnly over the mat, and say together, ' God Almighty,' and the priest answers, ' A pair of Micks,' which means that the offerings are not accepted, or he may say, ' Oh Lord, he has done 'em again,' and the joyful cries of some of the worshippers show that Allah is pleased, and so they, too, are glad."

On September 30, 1918, when the Australian and New Zealand ex-Cameliers blocked the road and railway to the Barada Gorge forming the exit from Damascus to the north, they intercepted a train carrying away large supplies of Turkish money both in gold coins and in paper notes. A quantity of the gold was commandeered before the rest was put securely under a guard, but the paper money was made common property. Men stuffed their pockets and saddle-bags with notes of all denominations, and pictured to themselves the pleasure awaiting them when they got leave to Damascus. But the first party to visit the town found that the notes were of no more value than blank pieces of paper, as the tradespeople would not accept them at all. Some use had to be made of the deflated money, so the "wealthy" soldiers broke into an orgy of card-playing for high stakes. The sky was the limit on a single throw at two-up or a hand at poker. One player would casually bet a hundred pounds on three aces, and the next player would calmly say, "Your hundred, and up another hundred," and the stakes would ultimately stagger even the Jubilee Plunger had he been present. Thousands of pounds would change hands at a sitting. The troopers would rise from a game, after having lost or won the price of a farm or sheep station, as serenely as if they were multi-millionaires, and no one was any the worse or the better for it. A hundred piastre note twisted into a squill would be used as a pipe lighter by a winner, and a loser would remark plaintively, " Well, that's the last of my ten thousand."

CHAPTER XXI

THE BIG BREAK THROUGH

In preparation for the next big movement the whole of the Australian Division was now armed with swords, and while the Light Horsemen were being trained in the use of the *arme blanche,* the New Zealand ex-Cameliers transferred their attention from camels, rifles, and Lewis guns, to horses and Vickers machine-guns. During the strenuous days of the next move their minds no doubt often reverted to the comforts they enjoyed in their old corps.

While the new Brigade was being trained for the part it was to take in the next military operations, General Allenby was training the minds of the Turkish leaders to misread his intentions regarding his next big movement. On previous occasions General Allenby's blows had been struck on the flank of his army on which the Cavalry Divisions were placed, so it was necessary to impress on the minds of the Turks that the Cavalry were in force in the Jordan Valley. For this purpose dummy horse-lines filled with dummy horses were set up near empty camps for the benefit of the Turkish aerial observers. Horse covers, or even light scrim stretched on a few light poles formed the bodies, while sand-bags, with pointed ears, and stuffed with hay, made quite presentable horses' heads when viewed from a height in the air. At the same time the one Mounted Division left in the valley, the Anzac Mounted Division under Major-General Chaytor, made a series of demonstrations so as to induce the enemy to believe that another attack across the Jordan was planned.

Any fresh troops arriving in the Jordan Valley came by day, the only ones to come were two battalions of the

Where the Mounted Forces were supposed to be

Where the Mounted Forces really were

Nablus

Tiberias and Sea of Galilee

Royal Fusiliers (Jewish Battalions, nicknamed the Jordan Highlanders), and two battalions of the British West Indies Regiment (B.W.I.), while all outward movements took place by night. The latter included the transfer of the Australian Mounted Division, the Fourth Cavalry Division, and the 60th Infantry Division from the extreme right of the line in the Jordan Valley to the extreme left on the coastal plain near the Mediterranean Sea. New camps were laid out in the Jordan Valley where the tents could catch the eyes of the Turkish observers in the air, but the supposed occupants were fifty miles away, although their bivvy fires still appeared to gleam brightly in the darkness every night, while transport vehicles, or even teams of mules drawing bundles of scrub here and there in the valley, literally raised clouds of dust in the air, which helped to figuratively throw dust in the eyes of the Turks. When the British preparations were completed in September, three cavalry and five infantry divisions were concealed in the orange and olive groves and plantations in the coastal plain and within fifteen miles of the front line, while over three hundred guns of all sizes were also concentrated on that flank instead of about seventy which were usually placed there.

Fast's Hotel, a large modern building erected on the Jaffa Road, outside the western wall of Jerusalem not far from the Jaffa Gate, was suddenly emptied of all its occupants, guards were put in charge of it, and the rumour was circulated that the whole building was required immediately for the Advanced Headquarters of the Commander-in-Chief. This rumour *was* intended to reach Turkish ears, and no doubt it did so.

That all these plans bore fruit is proved by Turkish documents captured after the big break through. In an enemy map issued the day before the advance of the British force, three of our infantry divisions and two cavalry divisions are shown in entirely wrong positions in the British territory, while their captured aeroplane reports state at the same time that, " no essential changes had taken place in the distribution of the British forces."

After darkness had fallen on the night of September 18, the troops moved to their allotted positions, like competitors in a race getting into their places to make a fast break-away when the starting signal was given. Everything was done by the clock, and it was most essential that each unit should move exactly at the time laid down for it, otherwise the whole great movement might be held up, or delayed for hours. As brigade after brigade filed into their respective positions, one could not help marvelling at the wonderful organizing work of the staff that had provided for all these movements, and worked out the time-table for each unit.

At 4.30 a.m. on September 19 the startled Turks were awakened by the crash of over three hundred British guns pouring their iron hail on the enemy's trenches near the coast. An intense bombardment of a quarter of an hour was followed by infantry attacks. The 60th Division next to the sea swept aside all opposition, and moved north up the plain, while the 7th, 75th, and Third Divisions, breaking the enemy line in front of them, swung round to the right, and forced the right flank of the Turks back into the hills.

At daylight on the 19th, every telephone centre and every aerodrome behind the Turkish armies were heavily and systematically bombed by our air force, which completely disorganized the signal communications of the enemy, so the Turkish Headquarters, fifty miles back at Nazareth, was completely ignorant of what was happening in its front line.

The way had been opened for the cavalry. The Fifth Cavalry Division swept directly north, followed closely by the Fourth Cavalry Division, and by evening

these forces were twenty-five miles from their starting
point of that morning. The Australian Mounted Division (less the newly formed Fifth A.L.H. Brigade) left
its camping ground near Ludd that same morning and
followed up the coastal plain. The objective of these
three cavalry divisions, now that they had left the
Turkish front line well behind them, was to press on at
utmost speed through the hills of Samaria, seize the
passes leading to the Plain of Esdraelon, spread down
the Valley of Jezreel to the Jordan, and so effectively
cut off the retreat of the Seventh and Eighth Turkish
armies when our infantry had driven them from their
front line positions.

In selecting the route for the cavalry, General Allenby
had the same problem to decide as confronted the
Egyptian Pharaoh, Thothmes III, in the year 1479 B.C.,
before the Israelites entered the Promised Land, when he
led his army through the same country to meet the army
of the kings of Syria and Palestine which awaited him
on the Plain of Esdraelon on the northern side of the
mountain passes. After this long interval of time, nearly
thirty-four centuries, an account of Thothmes's council
of war has been discovered in Egypt, probably the
earliest recorded account of such a nature in the world.
"They (the officers) spoke in the presence of His
Majesty, 'How is it that we should go upon this road
(the narrow Musmus Pass) which threatens to be narrow, while they come and say that the enemy is there
waiting, holding the way against a multitude? Will not
horse come behind horse, and man behind man likewise?
Shall our vanguard be fighting while our rearguard is
standing yonder in Aruna, not having fought? There
are yet two other roads; one road, behold it comes forth
at Taanach (the present road through Jenin), the other,
behold it will bring us upon the way north of Zefti, so
that we shall come out to the north of Megiddo (the

one through Abu Shushe). Let our victorious lord proceed upon the road he desires, but cause us not to go by
a difficult road.'" They were in favour of exercising
caution, but Thothmes believed in surprise tactics. "I
swear," he said, "as Ra loves me, as my father Amen
favours me, as my nostrils are filled with satisfying life,
My Majesty will proceed upon this road of Aruna. Let
him who will among you come in the following of My
Majesty. Shall they think, among those enemies whom
Ra detests, 'Does His Majesty proceed upon another
road? He begins to be fearful of us,' so will they think,"
and " He went forth at the head of his army himself,
showing the way by his own footsteps, horse behind
horse, His Majesty being at the head of the army."[1]
Thothmes surprised his enemies, and won a complete
victory.

And now in 1918, General Allenby, also using surprise tactics, poured a division of cavalry through this
same pass, which anticipated by an hour or two the
arrival of a Turkish force sent by Liman von Sanders
to occupy the position. The three British Cavalry Divisions seized all the strategic points from Haifa on the
coast to the Jordan River, captured railway rolling stock,
aeroplanes, artillery, and military stores of all descriptions, and proceeded to collect as prisoners the fragments
of the broken Seventh and Eighth Turkish armies as
they endeavoured to escape to the north.

In addition to the magnificent performance of the
cavalry force in advancing over fifty miles of enemy
country in twenty-four hours, an attempt was made of
such a sensational nature which, if it had been successful,
would have been handed down as an outstanding feat
in the annals of the British army. When the Plain of
Esdraelon was reached by the cavalry, a raid was made
on Nazareth to attempt to capture the Turkish

[1] *The Amarna Age,* Baikie (A. and C. Black) Ltd.

Commander-in-Chief, Marshall Liman von Sanders, and his staff, in their Headquarters fifty miles behind the main Turkish army which was still holding its front line position in the Judaean Mountains. At dawn on September 20, the 13th Cavalry Brigade was detached from the Fifth Cavalry Division, and entered Nazareth soon after daybreak. Liman von Sanders, still in ignorance as to what was happening to his Seventh and Eighth Armies, was awakened by the news that the British were entering the town, and he is said to have hurriedly departed in a motor car, clad only in his night attire.

CHAPTER XXII

TUL KERAM TO TIBERIAS

THE ex-Cameliers, the Fifth A.L.H. Brigade with its Second N.Z. Machine-gun Squadron, had been detached from the Australian Division, and attached to the 21st Corps, along with the French Cavalry Detachment, the Regiment Mixte de Marche de Cavalerie (R.M.M.C.), whose fantasic uniforms formed a marked contrast to the khaki of the Colonial Mounted Forces.

During the darkness of the night of September 18, the Brigade had moved into its allotted position. There was a feeling of tenseness among all ranks, as they waited for daylight and the signal to start on what was to be the greatest adventure of the whole campaign. Their training camp had been on the main Jaffa-Ludd road, and every night for weeks, from darkness till dawn, that road had seen a continuous procession of men, horses, guns and transport, all moving towards the coastal area. They knew by this time that they were a unit in perhaps the biggest cavalry force operating together, that had ever assembled in any war.

The horses and men were fit, the equipment was complete to the last buckle; orders were to move forward with all speed, and anyone who had the bad luck to fall out by the way, had to be left to his own devices. While travelling as light as possible (not even a blanket being carried), each horse was carrying in the neighbourhood of twenty stone, as it was expected to outdistance the wheeled transport during the next twenty-four hours.

The Brigade's mission was to gain at all speed a certain objective which was twenty miles away from its starting point.

The roar of the British artillery at 4.30 a.m. on the 19th, made known to all ranks that the big movement had begun. The Brigade moved off and crossed the River Auja at the allotted ford, which indicated that the guns and infantry had been successful in the first phase. Then a big delay while wire was cut, and trenches filled in; then away at a brisk trot through devastated trenches, dead and wounded men, abandoned equipment and guns, and all the vast carnage and waste of war.

Every now and then parties of Turks were encountered fighting a hasty rearguard action. The face of a shrapnel-swept spur of a hill was traversed at a gallop, the guns, ammunition-boxes, and gear of the gunners rattling on the pack-horses, and the swords of the Light Horsemen clanking at their horses' flanks. They were passing over the same ground on which on another September day in the year A.D. 1191 Richard the Lion Heart of England, with an army of 100,000 Crusaders had defeated 300,000 Saracens under their renowned leader Saladin. But Richard on his march from Haifa to Jaffa was able to move at the rate of only three miles a day.

There was no stand up fight for the Fifth Brigade until well on in the afternoon, but merely sharp bursts of rifle fire on the flank. At length the town of Tul Keram, the Headquarters of the Eighth Turkish army, came in sight. As the hasty retirement of the Turks in trains and lorries in the direction of Messudie could be seen, the French Colonial Cavalry was detached to pursue a battery of guns retiring from the town. Away they flung in a wild gallop, the multi-coloured Arab stallions that they rode, together with the weird head-dresses and cloaks of the Spahis, making an ever to be remembered sight. The Turkish battery attempted to wheel into action as this spectacular regiment dashed at them, but the gunners, in the act of serving the guns, were cut down as these fearless horsemen dashed among them, their big fair-haired lieutenant in the forefront actually beheading one gunner as he closed the breach of his gun.

Now up the hills on the opposite side of the town scrambled the Brigade, while overhead roared the aeroplanes of our forces, mercilessly bombing and machine-gunning the retreating enemy. As one flight of planes exhausted their supplies of bombs and ammunition, and tore away to their base to refill, another flight appeared out of the blue, and repeated the dose. In the gorge the scene of carnage was indescribable. In sheer desperation hundreds of Turks threw away their arms, and ran towards our Brigade, realizing that here only was there safety from these war birds which swooped down almost between the high sides of the gorge, and raked the enemy ranks with the fire of their machine-guns.

In Tul Keram itself an enemy force still offered resistance, no doubt trying to cover the retreat of the main body up the gorge. A Light Horse troop galloped across to capture the railway station, but as they neared the town, Turks rushed from buildings on the high ground, and poured a withering fire into the ranks of the Light Horse; many riderless horses galloped away, including that of the officer of the troop. Retribution swiftly followed. Being on an equal height with the Turks across the gorge at a distance of about 1,900 yards, the New Zealand gunners quickly got the range, and as the Turks had left the shelter of the buildings, very few of them got back. The Light Horse troop was avenged tenfold.

Suddenly, spinning down the grade from the town came a railway hand-trolley manned by half a dozen Turks making a desperate effort to rejoin the main body. As their plight was so hopeless and the shooting so easy, a humane machine-gun officer poured a sharp burst of bullets into the ballast ahead of the fast travelling trolley. The effect was ludicrous. The Turks literally flung themselves off the trolley, and scrambled like rabbits into a culvert, while the trolley, left to its own devices, careered away into the gorge.

Prisoners accumulated so rapidly that they became an encumbrance, and Brigadier Onslow, gathering a large body of them together, sent them under the charge of a few Light Horsemen back to meet the oncoming infantry, who had made remarkable progress, and were now not far in the rear of the Light Horse Brigade. Three thousand prisoners in all were rounded up by the Brigade at Tul Keram, while quantities of guns, munitions, and transport vehicles, were also captured.

But other work awaited the Brigade. When the horses had been watered and fed, the Brigade moved off again at midnight, this time to strike across the hilly country to the north-east, to cut the railway line running north from Nablus, which was the main line of communication of the Turks with their rear. Only goat-tracks were in existence, and these wound their way round rocks, up and down rough hillsides, and crossed deep stony beds of wadis, but the long slender column pressed on through the darkness, till next morning it struck the Turkish railway line at Ajje, some twenty-five miles behind the Turks' front line. The railway line was destroyed, thus effectively blocking any railway communication between the enemy front line and the north, and the column, gathering in any parties of Turkish troops it encountered, returned safely by dusk on the 20th to Tul Keram without having suffered any casualties. The Air Force had previously severed the nerve lines leading from the brains of the Turkish army to the members of its body that carried out the commands of the brain, and now the main artery that had supplied the material supplies for these same members had also been cut, and so the whole body was rendered useless as an organized fighting force. Had

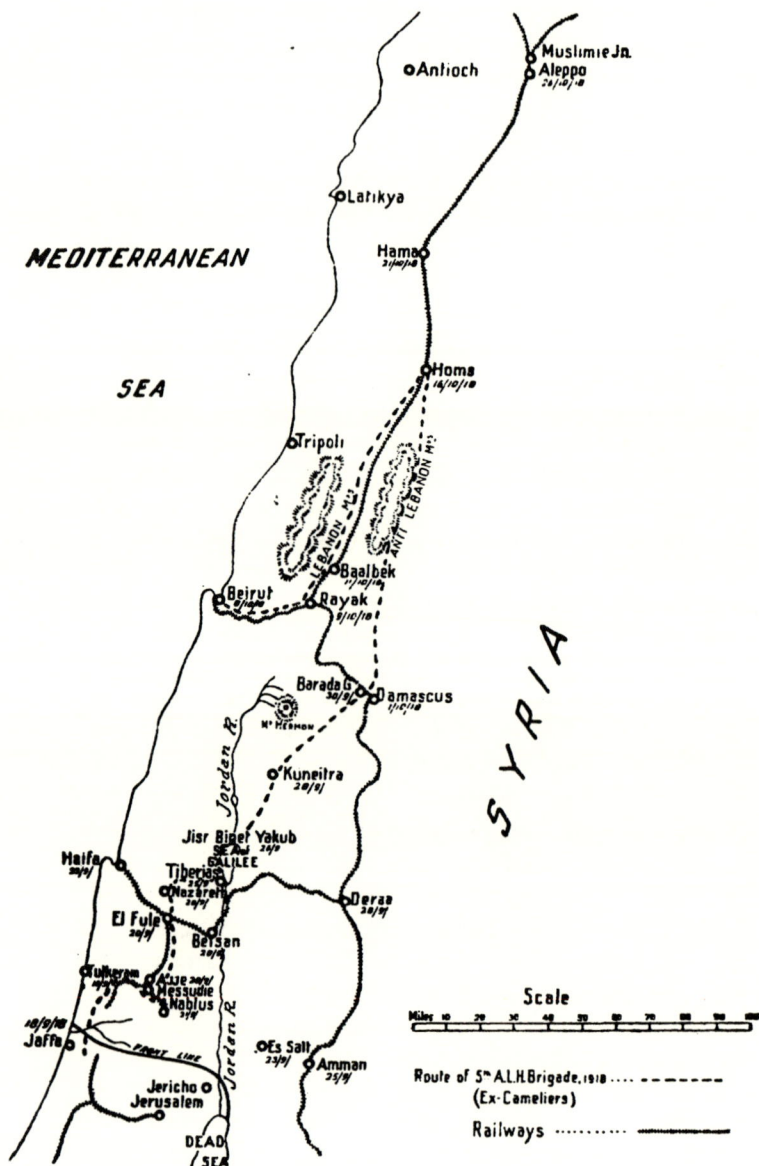

MEDITERRANEAN

SEA

SYRIA

Muslimie Jn.
Aleppo
26/10/18

Antioch

Latikya

Hama
31/10/18

Homs
16/10/18

Tripoli

ANTI LEBANON MTS

LEBANON MTS

Beirut
6/10/18

Baalbek
11/10/18

Rayak
5/10/18

Barada G.
30/9/18

Damascus
1/10/18

Mt Hermon

Kuneitra
28/9/18

Jordan R.

Jisr Binat Yakub
SE. Aul 26/9/18

GALILEE

Haifa
23/9/18

Tiberias
30/9/18

Nazareth
26/9/18

El Fule
20/9/18

Beisan
20/9/18

Deraa
28/9/18

Tulkeram
22/9/18

A'ure 20/9/18
Nessudie
Nablus
21/9/18

Jaffa
19/10/18

FRONT LINE

Es Salt
25/9/18

Amman
25/9/18

Jordan R.

Jericho
Jerusalem

DEAD
SEA

Scale

Miles 10   20   30   40   50   60   70   80   90   100

Route of 5th A.L.H.Brigade,1918 .... ― ― ― ―
(Ex-Cameliers)

Railways ········· ▬▬▬▬▬

210

the Turks any idea of the nature of this raid they could and would have made things very difficult for the Fifth Brigade.

Early on the morning of the 21st, the Brigade followed the road to Nablus which, situated fifteen miles behind the centre of the Turkish front line, had been the headquarters of the Seventh Turkish army during the last six months, and during that time our infantry had been unable to advance its line to any great extent owing to the rough nature of the country, and the determined resistance of the Turks. Now, however, the 53rd and 10th Divisions had driven back the enemy along the whole front of their sectors, and the Turks, pursued from the south by the 10th Division, were falling back by way of Nablus, and attempting to escape towards the north, or by way of the Wadi Fara, towards Jisr ed Damie, a bridge over the Jordan River, which was captured on the 22nd by Chaytor's Force (included in which was the N.Z.M.R. Brigade), thus blocking the retreat of the enemy to the eastern side of the river.

After some sixty hours of continuous marching and fighting, the Fifth A.L.H. Brigade, on that sweltering day (21st), found the hot dusty limestone gorge from Tul Keram a most uninviting place, as the bodies of the victims of the bombing operations of our air force, men horses and oxen, had lain in this " Valley of Death " for about two days, and were still unburied. Having overcome the feeble resistance in the gorge, the Brigade at last came within sight of Nablus, the Shechem of the Old Testament, lying between Mounts Ebal and Gerizim, where Abraham had built the first altar after his arrival in the Promised Land.

Here the N.Z. Machine-gunners had some really interesting experiences. At extreme range they engaged the outer defences of the town. Working forward in relays well up on the rough rocky sides of the gorge,

211

the gunners magnificently handled their guns under most difficult conditions. At last, getting into effective range, they engaged a couple of Turkish field-guns which could be seen on the main street at the crest of the hill which is the entrance to the town. This action developed into a private duel. Covering each other, and now and again taking machine-gun swept corners at a hand gallop, the gunners closed the range to seven hundred yards, when the odds became in favour of our machine-guns, and the Turks gave up the contest. Meanwhile the Light Horsemen were working round on the slopes of Mt. Ebal, and were enfilading the garrison, while up the Jerusalem-Nablus road were advancing the men of the Irish Division. At regular intervals a long drawn out scream through the air was followed by an earth-shaking explosion as the heavy artillery to the south-ward dropped their high-explosive shells into the city. These were still falling on the Mt. Ebal side as the N.Z. Gunners, escorted by the French Cavalry, entered the town, riding triumphantly to the centre where a halt was made; horses were watered from the local copious supplies, and within a few minutes afterwards, the invaders were briskly trading with the natives, who were non-combatants, and looked on with indifference at the military proceedings, as if at a show put on for their benefit.

Nablus, the ancient Shechem of the Old Testament, is one of the few towns in Palestine that has a name of Greek or Roman origin. When the Roman Emperor, Vespasian, conquered the country in A.D. 67 the town was destroyed, and when later on it was rebuilt, it was named Flavia Neapolis in honour of the Emperor. The name Neapolis (new city) gradually became corrupted to Nablus. The town has had many and exciting experiences from the times of the Patriarchs, but never did it witness such a scene as on September 21, when the Turks retreated headlong through the town towards the north, followed closely by the Irish Division, and cut off from one line of retreat by the Australian, French and New Zealand Mounted men, while artillery thundered between the Mounts of Ebal and Gerizim (which once heard the voices of Joshua and the priests of the Israelites reciting the curses and the blessings as ordered by Moses), while from the air the British aeroplanes hailed down their devastating bombs and machine-gun bullets that destroyed troops and transport, and blocked with their debris the other line of retreat leading down the Wadi Fara to the Jordan Valley, making the Wadi another " Valley of Death."

Lying on the ground that night at Balata the troops of the Fifth Brigade were grateful to the heavy artillery of the 10th Division, which did outpost duty by dropping an occasional shell in the direction of the disorganized retiring foe.

Moving north to Jenin next day, the Brigade discovered why no enemy aeroplanes had troubled it so far. These machines had been kept on the ground by our air force until the arrival of the Third A.L.H. Brigade which found twenty-four Turkish planes burned in their aerodromes. It is said that an amusing incident happened on the plain outside Jenin. A German doctor had remained at his post tending the wounded, until he saw the Light Horse charging down on the town. Hastily mounting a horse, he galloped away to try to catch up with the retreating forces. One of our airmen, in a spirit of deviltry, pursued him, swooping low over him and terrifying his horse so much that the poor beast collapsed in terror. The doctor continued on foot, and ran across an open space towards the Afule road, the airman still harassing him by putting a few bursts of machine-gun fire around him, until at last the doctor gave in, and stood and shook his fist and sword at the airman, then turned and walked back to the approaching Light Horsemen, to whom he freely expressed his opinion about our mad air force.

On the 24th of the month the Fifth Brigade moved north to Zerin on the Plain of Esdraelon where it rejoined the Australian Division with which it was to take part in the forthcoming sweep north into Syria. At Zerin was a great pool fed by a huge gushing spring of the purest water, which pours from a cave in the hillside. This is probably the same pool near which Saul's army camped before its defeat by the Philistines, when Saul and his three sons were killed. How the horses of our men revelled in it. Jaded men and horses waded into it, and enjoyed to the full one of the brightest interludes of the strenuous days they were passing through. What a different picture these khaki clad Colonials and their horses made from that seen, as is supposed, at this same pool, when Gideon of old tested his army of 10,000 selected men by a " drinking test," and reduced them to 300 for a night attack on the Midianites and Amalekites, " who lay along this same valley like grasshoppers for multitude, and their camels were without number, as the sands by the seaside for multitude." But our boys, always keen sports, recked not of the ancient history of the spot, or of the doings here of heroes of old, but, after seeing that their horses were thoroughly satisfied, set to work to try to catch the small fish which were present in the pool in large numbers, improvising nets from the material that had been issued to them for mosquito-netting. They little knew that they were following the example of the Crusaders, who are said to have been miraculously fed for three days on the fish caught in the springs at this place.

What a procession of warring forces ever since the dawn of recorded history have marched to battle on this

Plain of Esdraelon—Egyptians and Canaanites, Assyrians and Persians, Israelites and Philistines, Greeks, Romans and Jews, Saracens and Crusaders, Turks, Arabs and French have all in their turn, striven for mastery here, and now the scattered remnants of an Eastern army, which four days ago, with its modern equipment of aeroplanes, artillery and motor transport, had occupied an apparently impregnable position fifty miles to the south, were being gathered in in their thousands, with almost no loss to the conquerors, by an army organized and equipped in far off lands, and transported over thousands of miles of ocean.

If some magical power could call together the countless numbers who, through all the centuries of the past, from the scattered lands of the east and west, had fought together on this small plain, and could marshal them together in their diverse costumes, with their varied weapons of war, what an assembly it would be. No other level space of ground of equal size on the surface of the earth, could muster such a gathering of the harvest of war. Is it to be wondered at that the writer of the Book of Revelation should select this plain as the site of the battle of Armageddon, the final battle between the forces of good and evil? It is from Megiddo, the supposed site of Armageddon, that Lord Allenby has taken his title, Viscount Allenby of Megiddo.

But this district has a greater interest than as a battlefield for contending armies. In a humble carpenter's home in a small town overlooking this same plain, was reared the Son of Man, Whose influence over the world, more than nineteen hundred years after He died, still outweighs the influence of all the kings, and all the armies that fought for mastery throughout the ages on that plain within sight of Nazareth.

On again moved the Fifth Brigade, through the junction station of El Fule, with its abandoned railway yard full of stores, transport, and jumble of equipment, up the steep winding road fringed with capsized lorries, and simply littered with papers, no doubt records which the Turkish H.Q. Staff were trying to save when so swiftly overtaken by the Indian Lancers. And so the Brigade passed through the streets of Nazareth, of sacred memories. It was moonlight, and the ancient city was sleeping peacefully among the hills, and it was not without a little doubt as to the propriety of the proceedings that some of the troops dismounted and " commandeered " bags of barley from a mill, but their gallant horses were ever their first consideration.

Serious thoughts ever kept passing through the minds of thoughtful troopers as they passed these places of Biblical interest, and even the unlettered wished to know the stories attached to these towns. As a Brigade was passing through Nazareth, a padre remarked to the men in the section beside which he happened to be, " It is very interesting to see this old town, my lads." " What place is this, padre? " queried a Light Horseman. " Oh, this is Nazareth," replied the padre as he prepared to push on. " Hey, padre, hold on," called the trooper. " What's the strength of this 'ere Nazareth joint? " In an idiom well known to all ranks he was merely asking what was the history of Nazareth.

On moved the Mounted Force across the battlefield where in 1187 King Guy, the Christian King of Jerusalem, and practically the whole of his knights and followers were captured or slain by Saladin and his Saracens, thus putting an end to the Crusaders' hopes in Palestine.

The Division made a halt during the night of the 25th at Kefr Kenna, the Cana of the New Testament, where the miracle of changing wine into water was performed at the wedding feast, but no wine or wedding feasts were apparent to our troops that night. Perhaps any intended weddings were postponed indefinitely when the Australians and New Zealanders were seen approaching.

On the evening of September 26 the troops gazed down on ancient Tiberias, nestling by the side of the beautiful sea of Galilee. Down the winding road moved the Division. From a thousand feet above sea-level it quickly dropped down until it reached the shores of Galilee, over six hundred feet below sea-level. And into the lake rode the troops up to their horses' flanks, for Galilee water is as sweet and fresh as that of the Dead Sea is bitter and salt.

A novel encounter took place at the south end of the Sea of Galilee, near Semakh, where the German machine-gunners put up such a desperate resistance to the men of the Fourth A.L.H. Brigade. When Semakh was finally overcome, some German gunners attempted to escape in a motor boat, but were pursued by one of our fighting aeroplanes. The boat was armed with machine-guns, and after our airman had missed with a couple of bombs, a duel with machine-guns took place between the Galilee navy and a British aeroplane actually flying below sea-level. The plane won.

CHAPTER XXIII

THE RACE FOR DAMASCUS

ON September 22, as recorded in the Official History of the Australians in the War, Volume III, General Allenby visited Lieut.-General Chauvel, G.O.C. Desert Mounted Corps, at Megiddo. Both agreed that the three days' operations had far exceeded their hopes. They had contemplated heavy fighting at Jenin and Beisan, and would not have been surprised if considerable forces of Turks had broken through the cavalry line, and established a strong resistance to any further advance towards Damascus.

" What about Damascus? " he asked Chauvel, who replied laconically, " Rather."

On the morning of the 25th, Allenby met the three Corps Commanders, Lieut.-Generals Chauvel, Chetwode, and Bulfin, in conference at Jenin, and as a result an immediate advance on Damascus was decided on. This meant that new arrangements had to be made immediately for the transport of all necessary supplies for three cavalry divisions moving at top speed. The port of Haifa had been captured and could be used as a fresh base, and it is a splendid tribute to the organizing officers of the force that these divisions were able to start next morning.

And now began the last desperate race between the British and Turkish forces, for which the prizes were to be Damascus, the oldest existing city in the world, a hundred miles away, and beyond that, Aleppo, two hundred miles farther on. When had there been such a contest? A race of three hundred miles, the competitors to be mounted divisions and motor transport columns on the outside running, while on the direct course was the retreating Fourth Turkish Army, followed by our

Fourth Cavalry (Indian) Division and the Arabs of the Sheriffian Army under Feisul and Lawrence.

Chaytor's Force, including the N.Z. Mounted Brigade, had blocked the passages over the lower and middle Jordan, and had advanced eastward across the river through Es Salt to Amman which was captured on September 25, by the Anzac Mounted Division. The Second Turkish Army which was retiring north from Maan, was intercepted by this Division, which in ten days captured over ten thousand prisoners and fifty-five guns.

On September 26 three Mounted Divisions started on their sweep north from Galilee. The Fourth Cavalry Division crossed the Jordan south of the Sea of Galilee, and made its way across difficult hilly country to Deraa at the junction of the Palestine railway line with the Hedjaz railway from Damascus to Medina. There it linked up with the Sheriffian forces, and followed up the retiring Turks in the direction of Damascus.

The Australian Mounted Division, followed by the Fifth Cavalry Division, was despatched up the west side of the Sea of Galilee, to strike north-east across the high tableland with the object of reaching Damascus before the Fourth Turkish Army could arrive there. All ranks now guessed what their next objective was, and welcomed the endurance test ahead of them. They felt that they had, during the last seven days, completely established their superiority over the enemy under whatever circumstances they encountered him.

The Fifth A.L.H. Brigade with its N.Z. Gunners led the advance of the Division along the side of the Galileean Lake of sacred memories. The waters of the lake, sparkling in the sunlight on their right flank, gave a completely different aspect to the campaign. Here was water, cool, fresh, and clear, in abundance. No longer need man or horse suffer from thirst or dust, or feel that a wash was too expensive a luxury to be indulged in. In high spirits rode the mounted men past the sites of ancient Bethsaida and Capernaum, formerly flourishing towns (whose ruins now proved the accuracy of Christ's direful prophecy), and on past the northern end of the lake until they reached the vicinity of the bridge over the Upper Jordan River which flows down from the southern slopes of Mount Hermon through the marshes of Hule, or Waters of Merom, into the northern end of the Sea of Galilee. This bridge, called Jisr Binat Yakub (the Bridge of the Daughters of Jacob), carried the traffic to the high plateau at Kuneitra which was the jumping-off place for Damascus.

Fighting a desultory rearguard action during the afternoon, the Turks managed to delay the advance long enough to allow them to evacuate a village which they occupied as a repair depot for transport vehicles, and retiring to the eastern side of the river, they blew up one of the masonry arches of the bridge. This was a serious check to the mounted men who were racing against time to reach the distant goal ahead. The Turkish machine-gunners held the steep rocky slopes of the opposite bank, and as two divisions of cavalry were following up in the track of the Fifth Brigade, the latter had at all costs to effect a crossing over the Jordan. During the late afternoon the N.Z. guns and the mitrailleuses of the French regiment and some guns of the other L.H. Brigades were massed on the west bank, and during the night kept up a heavy counter-fire against those of the enemy. While they were thus engaged, the Fourth and Fifth Brigades succeeded in making a crossing in the darkness of night under extremely difficult conditions lower down the stream. The banks were steep and high, and were composed of rocks and rounded stones; the horses found great difficulty in getting a footing, and had often to be assisted up the bank with ropes round their hindquarters, the troopers pulling them up by sheer strength. It was a splendid piece of work carried out under almost incredible conditions, but the Jordan was crossed, and the Turkish force completely outflanked.

Early next morning the remainder of the ex-Cameliers crossed the river for the last time. Six months before they had crossed and recrossed it near its mouth at the Dead Sea; they had held outpost on its banks, and bathed in its waters in its middle course; and now, in view of the mountains whose snows supplied it with water, they were to say farewell to it.

Already the engineers had effected sufficient temporary repairs to allow of our artillery and transport to cross. No sooner were they across and winding up amongst the rounded boulders than an enemy aeroplane appeared, and to the huge delight of our men, proceeded to bomb the place we had evacuated two hours before. Then he spotted the teeming road full of horses and men, and turning, swooped down with his guns barking spitefully at them. A section of the New Zealanders perched two machine-guns on rocks to get elevation, and with two men to each gun holding them in position and feeding the ammunition belts in, our gunners gave battle to this grim bird of war. He soon made off after doing little or no damage. Shortly after the drone of one of our planes was heard coming from the direction of Haifa. He disappeared towards Damascus; an hour passed, and he returned, circled round the Division, and dropped the laconic message, " Got him."

The country northward from the Upper Jordan is covered with loose stones and boulders which proved very trying to the horses and motor transport, but in spite of these difficulties the column pushed on past Deir es Saras, where the Third L.H. Brigade captured prisoners and guns, and at nightfall on the 28th the Division arrived at Kuneitra. On the afternoon of the

29th, the advance was continued, the Third L. Horse leading. Strong opposition was met with at Sasa, which was captured in the darkness of the early morning by the Eighth and Ninth A.L.H. Regiments, when many prisoners, all the enemy machine-guns, and two field pieces were taken.

From early morn on the 30th, dense columns of smoke could be seen in the distance ahead, indicating that the Turks realized that it was impossible to stem the irresistible force of this well-ordered mass of swiftly moving, hard-fighting horsemen who had carried all before them since the artillery and infantry had opened the gate for them to pass through ten days before. Halting for breakfast the Commanding Officer of Desert Mounted Corps issued his final orders to Divisional and Brigade leaders, and the stage was set for the final dash and assault which was to result in the ancient " Garden City " passing from the rule of the Turk.

The country was at first rough and rocky, but soon after Sasa was passed, the plain opened out level and clear. It was a situation for cavalry and the opportunity was immediately seized. *Military Operations, Egypt and Palestine,* vividly describes what followed: " The Australian Light Horsemen made the pace a cracker, breaking up into small parties, and rounding up fugitives. The Australians were unshaven and dusty, with eyes bloodshot from lack of sleep, but rode with the bursting excitement of schoolboys. Their blood tingled with the sheer joy of their gallop to victory, and they laughed aloud as they thundered down on the terrified enemy. With swords flashing in the early sunrise, little parties of three and four men raced shouting on bodies of Turks ten and twenty times their number."

Later on in the morning Turkish forces some thousands strong with their transport were seen six miles across the plain, retiring on Damascus, and in an attempt to check our force, they took up a position on the ridges on either side of Kaukab, on the Kuneitra-Damascus road. (Kaukab is said to be the spot where Paul, breathing out threatenings and slaughter against the disciples of the Lord, was suddenly converted and called to the apostleship.) But no check was allowed to stop the advance of the mounted men. Bouchier's Force (Fourth and Twelfth A.L.H. Regiments) was detailed to attack this position with the sword, while the Third and Fifth L.H. Brigades raced away to the north-west to isolate Damascus on the north by blocking the two roads leading to Beirut and Homs. Heavy shell and machine-gun fire was encountered at El Mezze, but this was soon silenced by our artillery, and Langley's Regiment (14th L.H.) outflanked the Turks, and pushed on for the hills overlooking Damascus from the north-west.

The tall spires of the minarets of mosques, together with the huge latticed masts of the wireless station, could be seen rising above the trees and gardens which surrounded the great city, while more fires could be seen rising from the enormous dumps which existed in and around the town. Some sort of resistance was offered from the shelter of gardens, but this was more in the nature of a delay than of an action. Branching away diagonally to the left, the Fifth Brigade and N.Z. Gunners pushed well forward of the central attack. Here the incident of Nablus was almost repeated, when two of our machine-guns engaged two Turkish field-guns both in view of each other. But time being the essence of the contract, our force streamed away still farther to the left, the land rising as it advanced. Any feeble, unorganized opposition was brushed aside, and when opportunity offered, looking away to the right, our men saw, miles behind them, a disorganized rabble, once the Fourth Turkish army, streaming along on the road from Deraa, and harassed continually by the shrapnel of the pursuing Fourth Cavalry Division, while our Arab allies hung on its flanks. It was the finish of the great race; all the competitors were in view, and our force was leading. Chauvel's plans with his driving power behind them, had been successfully carried out; all that remained to be done was to take possession of the prize, the vastness of which, as our Brigade advanced up the hillsides, spread out before it.

But the most dramatic episode of the campaign was still to follow. As the mounted men crossed the top of the ridge of the range north of the town, no sign of any road or railway could be seen. A sub-section of the New Zealand Machine-gunners under Lieut. Duncan was feeling its away along the hillside away from the city, when Sergeant Kirkpatrick, being convinced that the road must be close at hand, offered to reconnoitre to the right, and galloped down the steep stony hillside, when to his astonishment, the ground seemed to open suddenly in front of him, and he had just time to rein up his horse on the edge of a precipice overlooking a gorge, the verge of which, from a distance, had seemed to merge into the slopes of the hills on the opposite side. There below him, at the bottom of the cliff, was a river, a railway, and a road on which was packed a retreating Turkish army numbering thousands of men, with transport vehicles of all descriptions, while a heavily laden train was also steaming north on the railway line beside the road. Both sides of the narrow gorge were precipitous, so that there was no way of escape. The only description of the situation that entered Kirkpatrick's mind were the words of Cromwell, "The Lord has delivered them into our hands." The little party of machine-gunners at once took command of the situation, and placing their guns in position, they poured in both on the front and on the rear of the enemy column, a stream of death through which neither man nor beast

A section of Second N.Z.M.G.S.

Jisr Binat Yakub Bridge

Barada Gorge, September, 1918

Barada Gorge, 1919

could pass. A heavily laden train was also attended to as it struggled up the grade. Sweeping it at a steep angle, the machine-guns ripped the roofs of the cars. Some vehicles at the rear were detached by the Turkish soldiers to enable the front portion of the train to get away, but the accurate gun-fire from the hilltop made this quite impossible. The troops in the rear of the retreating mass, unaware of the blockage in front, kept pressing forwards, while those in front tried in terror to force their way back from the devastating fire ahead. Bullock-carts, motor cars, gharries, hand-carts, motor lorries, ammunition waggons, limbers, camels, horses, and field-kitchens were inextricably mixed up. Confusion reigned in the gorge until at last the whole column was halted. Beginning at the Damascus end of the gorge, the Turkish soldiers were made to about turn, and leave the gorge, when over four thousand surrendered *en masse* to the Australians.

It was far on in the following day ere the living were all removed from that scene of carnage, and much arduous and unpleasant work had to be accomplished before the road became even passable for mounted and wheeled traffic. Long will the dreadful sights of that otherwise beautiful gorge live in the memories of those who saw it on that morning of October 1, 1918.

But this overwhelming victory of General Allenby's, conceived so boldly, and developed and executed so swiftly, was to have a most appropriate spectacular finale before the curtain was finally rung down on the last scene, the capture of Damascus. At the end of that last day of September, there was staged on the outskirts of the ancient city, a display of fireworks of such a nature as had never before been seen in the Holy Land, or perhaps in any land.

When the Turkish Commanders realized that complete disaster had overwhelmed their forces, they ordered the destruction of everything that might be of use to the victorious invaders. Earlier in the afternoon of the 30th, while the disorganized remnants of the Turkish Fourth Army were still streaming in from the south, harried by the Arab forces, and raked by shrapnel from the British Fourth Cavalry Division, a tremendous explosion shook the hills, and the tall latticed masts of the powerful wireless station on the outskirts of the city swayed and toppled to the ground. Then followed the destruction of the buildings which housed the generating power for the station. With a mighty roar, the roof seemed to rise in the air, and scatter machinery and instruments over the neighbourhood. The destruction of the station meant that communication to the outside world from Turkish Headquarters had ceased. One wondered what was the last despairing message sent out over the air before this final acknowledgement of defeat was made to the world at large.

This destruction, impressive though it was, was but the prelude of the spectacular and awe-inspiring closing scene. As the day drew to a close and the stuttering roar of the steaming machine-guns died down, and the rattling of rifle fire in the dreadful gorge of death ceased, there arose denser clouds of smoke and flame from the great dumps on the outskirts of the beleaguered city, where were stored immense supplies of petrol, shells, cartridges, and explosives of all descriptions, as well as fodder, tents, and all the necessary equipment for the supplies of the Turkish armies in Syria, Palestine, and Arabia.

As darkness fell, the flames spread rapidly amongst the inflammable material, and roar and crash succeeded each other with ever-increasing rapidity and intensity, until they seemed to merge into a continuous roll of thunder which echoed in the adjacent hills. Rows upon rows of great fifty and hundred gallon drums of petrol covered many acres of ground, and as the flames reached these, each one exploded, and sprayed its flaming contents over its neighbours, which in turn burst and hurled themselves hundreds of feet up in the air in great sheets of flame.

Close at hand to these were the great ammunition dumps which in their turn added their contribution to the vast inferno. As shells exploded high in the air, Verey lights in myriads of stars lent colours of every brilliant hue to the grandeur of the scene.

Hour after hour raged the thundering conflagration, lighting up as clearly as daylight, the age-old city and the surrounding plain with its verdant covering of trees, while farther away stood out the illuminated hills, gazing down on this gateway of the great Arabian Desert which stretched away to ancient Baghdad, while in the outer distance was the vast background of the darkness of the Eastern night.

From the very top of the highest hill overlooking the western entrance to Damascus, and distant about a mile and a half in an air line from the blazing inferno, the Australian Light Horsemen and the New Zealand Machine-gunners lay beside their tired horses and worn guns. Exhausted as they were with the strenuous days and sleepless nights they had spent in the mad race from Galilee, these Crusaders from the Southern Seas had all thought of fatigue banished from their minds by the immensity of the marvellous scene being enacted before them. They could not but feel that they were witnessing the death throes of a fighting nation which for centuries had held at bay the armed forces of Europe, and they grimly realized that the immense supplies of death-dealing explosives intended for the destruction of themselves, had provided the materials for the funeral pyre of the Turkish nation.

As the night wore on, the explosions became more fitful, and gradually they ceased altogether, and the tired soldiers huddled together on the bare hilltop, and dropped into well-earned slumber. Quietness descended on the hills and valleys, a quietness broken only by the sighing of a tired horse, or the distant cry of a prowling jackal in the hills, while overhead the cold blazing stars, which are nowhere so bright as in this ancient and romantic land, looked down on the scene as serenely as, for thousands of years, they had looked down on the succession of conquerors whom they had seen come and go, ever since the dawn of history.

CHAPTER XXIV

FINAL MOVEMENTS

At 6 a.m. on October 1, Wilson's Third A.L.H. Brigade rode into Damascus from the north while the Sheriffian force entered from the south. The Australians passed on to the north-east by the Homs road, and overtook another retiring force of Turks at Duma, Kusseir and Kubbeth i Asafir, capturing 1,500 prisoners and all their equipment. These engagements on September 30 and October 1 and 2 north of Damascus were the last serious encounters with the Turks, whose remaining forces consisted only of parties of troops in full retreat toward the north.

During the twelve days between September 19 and October 1, the Australian Division had advanced over a hundred and fifty miles. Its casualties during this time were twenty-one killed and seventy-one wounded, while the prisoners captured by it amounted to 31,335.

The ex-Cameliers during that hectic fortnight had lived and fought and ridden at such a pace, through so many interesting places of historic and Biblical fame that the mind was left bewildered by the wonder of it all. The tiring, sleepless rides, the desperate though spasmodic fighting, the daylight and the moonlight treks, the grim duels in pitch darkness, seemed so confusingly intermingled, that, after it was all over, it was difficult to place in the mind in anything like their proper sequence, the stirring events of the past fourteen days. But each man realized that he had taken part in one of the most successful and spectacular cavalry drives in the history of his nation, if not of the world.

Then came a brief period of inaction; camping in the Barada Gorge, the Brigade, like a wounded animal, rested in its lair, and as it were, licked its wounds.

During this period rain fell, and the weather became colder, and as, during the exciting days of the preceding fortnight, men and horses had been drawing on their reserve strength, so it was not surprising that a reaction set in. Many men had become infected with malaria germs, and now, no longer buoyed up by excitement, gave way to the dread disease. Evacuations to hospital became more and more frequent, until there were scarcely enough men left to carry out the necessary camp duties. It was no uncommon sight to see officers, n.c.o's and troopers alike, leading as many as seven horses apiece to water. One troop at this stage was reduced to one officer and one sergeant. The horses, too, gallant creatures that they were, became emaciated and dispirited, and it was a touching sight to see the men, who had such a genuine affection for their mounts, searching along the gorge and up the side wadis for bits of "bukshee" fodder, and tit-bits for them. A patch of sugar-cane discovered in the vicinity soon became a casualty.

The Fifth A.L.H. Brigade, along with the rest of the Australian Division, concentrated in and around Damascus until October 26, when it moved north by stages to Homs, over a hundred miles to the north, which it reached on the 31st, to act as reserve troops for the Fifth Cavalry Division which had moved by forced marches of mounted troops and armoured cars to Rayak, the railway junction with the Beirut railway, through Baalbek, Homs, and Hama, until it finally entered Aleppo on October 26, passing on two days later to Muslimie Station, the junction with the railway running from Constantinople towards Baghdad. Since leaving its starting-point on September 19, this Division had travelled a distance of over three hundred miles, and had captured over 10,000 prisoners.

View of Damascus

Strait Street, Damascus

Great Bazaar, Damascus

View of Baalbek

At noon of October 31 the Armistice between the Allies and Turkey came into force.

During November the New Zealand Second Machine-gun Squadron moved with the Fifth A.L.H. Brigade south to Baalbek, and for four months provided guards at Homs, Baalbek, and Rayak, until on March 4 they moved to Beirut, from which port they embarked in the *Ellenga* for Port Said.

When the N.Z. Machine-gunners arrived from Syria at the N.Z. Detail Camp at Chevalier Island, Ismailia, the natives of Egypt were still unsettled after the outbreak of the Egyptian Insurrection early in 1919, and in the middle of April, the squadron was sent to the town of Tanta on the railway to Alexandria, and patrolled part of the Delta as far as Zifta and Mehallal Kubra until June 20, when the majority of the men proceeded to Chevalier Island, and at the end of the month embarked on the Ulimaroa at Suez for the return to New Zealand. The remainder of the squadron, after handing in horses and equipment, followed a few weeks later in the *Ellenga*.

CHAPTER XXV

AN EX-CAMELIER AS EDUCATIONIST

"I HAVE had a peculiar experience in the war, Major," said an Australian officer to the writer one morning early in 1919, as we were strolling through the camp at Kantara on the Suez Canal, while waiting for the express train from Port Said to Cairo. " I left Australia with the Main Body as a Major in the Light Horse; I have been through the whole war from Gallipoli to the Armistice, and I am going back to Australia with the same rank as I had when I left. I don't think there is another senior officer who has not had promotion." " What was the matter with your O.C.? Would he not get in the road of a bullet or go sick? " I asked. " Yes, he was away several times, and I then had command of the regiment, but he always returned, and I had to revert to my original rank." " That is hard luck," I replied. " I can appreciate your feelings, as I have had rather a unique experience myself." " What was that? " asked the Australian. " At this time yesterday I was a trooper in the ranks." " Go to Hell," retorted the Aussie hotly. " But it is a fact," I said. " You are pulling my leg," he replied. " Oh no, I wouldn't try to pull your leg in the daylight." " How the devil did you do it?" he asked. " Just by pure merit," I replied. " Let me in on the joke," said he, so I explained. " By gad, that's the best thing I have heard of in the war. Good luck to you, old man," he exclaimed as he held out his hand. Two extremes in promotion in the E.E.F. had met by accident.

Towards the end of November, 1918, while convalescing in the N.Z. Detail Camp at Ismailia, I read in a New Zealand paper an account of the proposals for the education of the New Zealand troops in England and France. I asked a padre if anything was proposed to be done in this respect for our men in Egypt and Palestine. He had not heard of the proposals, and borrowed the paper. The next day the O.C. of the camp sent for me, and when he found that I was an Inspector of Schools in civil life, he asked me to outline a scheme for the men in the camp. A committee was set up by him, representing the various units, and the scheme was put before them and adopted. It was sent to N.Z. Headquarters for authority to finance it and put it into operation.

On December 11 the O.C. Camp received from Anzac Mounted Divisional H.Q. a telegram, " Forward Trooper Robertson, Second M.G.S., here for interview with G.O.C." On reaching Richon le Zion where the Division was camped, I found everything in a state of unrest as a result of the sacking of the neighbouring Bedouin village of Surafend as revenge for the murder of a New Zealand Machine-gunner. Following an interview with Major-General Chaytor, I returned to Ismailia, and organized educational classes there while the Division moved south to an uninhabited district near Rafa in the south of Palestine. At Richon there was a large wine factory, Christmas was drawing near, and after the incident at Surafend, and General Allenby's remarks thereon, it was considered advisable to remove the Australians and New Zealanders from the danger zone.

In the Detail Camp at Chevalier Island, Ismailia, sixteen different classes were provided. Attendance at lectures on economics, civics and hygiene was compulsory for all ranks; in other subjects a choice was allowed. The most popular classes were motor mechanics, wool-classing, stock-breeding, veterinary lectures, and book-keeping. Other subjects were English, arithmetic, electricity, commercial correspondence, shorthand, agriculture, farriery, building trade, and fruit-farming. No illiterate individuals were found in the ranks requiring elementary instruction.

When the Anzac Division was settled in its camp at Rafa on the exact site from which the New Zealand Mounted Brigade had launched its successful attack on the Turkish redoubt on January 9, 1917, I proceeded there by night train, arriving in the early morning. I was refused a lift either for myself or my kit by the driver of a motor lorry from H.Q., so had to tramp the two miles through the sand to the camp. Reporting at D.H.Q. Orderly tent, I was told by the D.A.A.G. to get badges and a Sam Browne belt, as I would be made a Sergeant-major.

At 10 a.m. I waited on General Chaytor who approved of the programme suggested for the N.Z. Brigade, and agreed to the appointment of the instructors recommended. Amongst these were university graduates, doctors, lawyers, school teachers, veterinary surgeons, accountants, engineers, and successful stock breeders. He informed me he would give me the rank of Major while I acted as Assistant Director of the Education Department of the N.Z.E.F.

When I retired the D.A.A.G. went in to see the General, and I waited till he returned. When he came back to the Orderly Tent he burst out, " Here's a blinking joke. I was going to make you a Sergeant-major and the General has made you a Major. He wants you to dine with him to-night." " I can't dine with a Major-General in a uniform like this," I objected. " Try on my tunic," he cried as he threw it off. " Fits you like a glove. I'll borrow a pair of crowns from Hemphill. You can buy a collar and tie at the canteen. Everything else is all right. You'll do."

Hygiene Class

Wool Classing

Motor Mechanics

T. Major J. Robertson,
A.D.E. to N.Z.M.R.

I was provided with a letter of introduction to Brigadier-General Meldrum whom I found in the afternoon, enjoying a cup of tea with two of his staff in the reed-walled messroom at Brigade H.Q. He read the letter solemnly, and then asked if I was Major Robertson. "I don't know, sir," I replied gravely. "I was Trooper Robertson half an hour ago." "Well, what will you have to drink, Major?" he asked as he shook hands, and then introduced me to his astonished companions.

At 7 p.m. I presented myself with the D.A.A.G. at D.H.Q. messroom where I had difficulty in advancing through a heavy barrage of kindly intentioned offers of "spots" from nearly everyone present. But as I had to dine with the General and his senior staff officers, all colonels, I dare not become a casualty, so outflanked the barrage safely. A motor car had been ordered by the General to be ready at 9 p.m. to take me to catch the night train for Cairo, and rumour had it that the car was driven by the same driver that had refused me a lift in the morning.

Work similar to that carried on at the Detail Camp was started with the Brigade, but as no buildings were available, the classes were all held out in the open air, the Instructor standing on a slight mound, and the men sitting on the sand in front of him. What a contrast this scene in the year A.D. 1919 made to that when 1,900 years before the Birth of Christ, the flocks of Abraham grazed over this same spot, but the land itself was in nowise altered since that remote period. Perhaps one of his shepherds, or even Abraham himself had stood on the same mound of sand to keep watch over his sheep, where now stood a graduate of Lincoln College, lecturing, to an armed force, on sheep-breeding in New Zealand.

These classes gave the men something to think and talk about, and took their minds off military matters, which they all hoped were things of the past. But on two half days every week lectures on such things as musketry, cleaning of arms, guard mounting, etc., were still carried on. The men did not take kindly to these, but the General insisted. He said the Brigade was still a fighting force in the field, and might be called on again for active service, and he proved to be right.

The Nationalist party in Egypt under Zaglul Pasha had planned an insurrection against the authority of the British, and a date had been appointed for the outbreak. The military authorities were aware of what was being planned, and before the date fixed they suddenly arrested Zaglul, and deported him to Malta. When Zaglul's arrest became known all Cairo was in an uproar. Mobs gathered in the streets and destroyed public and private property, and the whole country was put under martial law. All streets in Cairo except the principal ones were put out of bounds for all ranks, and the city was patrolled by mounted troops and armed motor lorries. In the country railway lines were broken up, stations were set on fire, telegraph lines destroyed, and a number of Europeans, including several British soldiers on leave up the Nile, were killed.

At midday on March 17, 1919, orders came to Rafa for the Anzac Mounted Division to proceed to Egypt to help to quell the revolt. By 5 p.m. the N.Z. Brigade was entrained for the Canal, and as its various units were placed in towns scattered over the Delta from Cairo to the sea, it was impossible to carry on educational work with it. Lectures were still carried on at the Detail Camp until the troops were embarked for New Zealand in July, 1919. On the voyage home various classes were carried out on the transports *Ulimaroa* and *Ellenga*.

AN EX-CAMELIER AS EDUCATIONIST

All ranks were sorry to say farewell to old and tried comradeships they had formed in the British and Australian forces throughout the stirring times on Gallipoli, in the Sinai Peninsula, and in Palestine and Syria, but stronger attachments drew them back to the peaceful islands in the far south, and when in August the shores of New Zealand were sighted, they began to realize that their period of warfare was over, and they eagerly looked forward to the welcome awaiting them in their own homes, and to returning once more to their peaceful occupations in civil life.

CHAPTER XXVI

IN MEMORIAM

Of all the fighting units in the British Army that took part in the Great War, the exploits of the Imperial Camel Brigade are probably least known to the general public. Yet this Brigade has a memorial set up in the heart of the Empire, on which are inscribed the names of all members of the force who gave their lives for their King and Country, and included in these are the names of six officers and thirty-five other ranks of the two New Zealand Companies which formed part of the Brigade.

The memorial consists of the bronze figure of a Camelier in complete marching order, mounted on a camel. On two sides of the square base are bronze reliefs depicting typical scenes in the life of the troopers in action, while on the front and the rear of the base are carved in bronze the names of three hundred and forty-six officers and men of the Corps who died during the campaign. On the lower part of the base are the words: " To the Glorious and Immortal Memory of the Officers, N.C.O's and Men of the Imperial Camel Corps—British, Australian, New Zealand, Indian—who fell in action or died of wounds and disease in Egypt, Sinai, and Palestine, 1916, 1917, 1918."

The monument stands in Victoria Gardens, on the Thames Embankment in London, and was unveiled in 1921, by Lieut.-General Sir Philip Chetwode, who commanded in its early career, Desert Column of which the Camel Corps formed a part. There were present at the ceremony, Brigadier-General C. L. Smith, v.c., m.c., who commanded the Brigade during the whole of its career, Colonel de Lancey Forth, O.C. of the Third (Australian) Battalion, Colonel R. V. Buxton, O.C. of the

*Memorial to Imperial Camel Corps,
Thames Embankment, London*

British Military Cemetery,
Mt. Scopus, overlooking Jerusalem

Second (British) Battalion, Major Lord Winterton, M.P., second in command of the Second Battalion, while Mr. Hughes on behalf of the Australian Government, and Mr. W. P. Massey on behalf of New Zealand also took part in the ceremony.

After a prayer of dedication had been offered, and floral tributes had been placed at the base of the memorial, seven pipers of the Scots Guards played the lament, " The Flowers of the Forest," and buglers sounded the " Last Post."

After the Armistice the Imperial War Graves Commission had the bodies of those who fell in the campaigns in Palestine and Syria, collected into the Military Cemeteries at Gaza, Deir el Belah, Beersheba, Ramleh, Haifa, Damascus, or Jerusalem.

The Military Cemetery at Jerusalem is situated on the top of Mt. Scopus about a mile and three-quarters to the north of the city. From this spot a commanding view of the Holy City and its surroundings is obtained. One gets a good idea of the rocky limestone ridge on which the city is built, and the outstanding buildings are seen in their natural relation to each other, the Temple Area, Haram esh Sheriff, in the midst of which stands the Moslem Mosque, the Mosque of Omar (the Dome of the Rock or Kubbet es Sakhra), which according to Arab historians was built by Abd el Melik in the ninth century, over the spot where Abraham is said to have prepared to offer up Isaac as a sacrifice. On this spot also David erected an altar, and here also the Temple of Solomon and the succeeding Jewish Temples were built. The Aksa Mosque, Mesjid el Aksa, the most distant mosque (from Mecca) in the south of the Temple Area, and the Church of the Holy Sepulchre, to which pilgrims from Christendom have directed their footsteps from the earliest times of the Christian era, stand out clearly.

It was on Mt. Scopus that Titus and his Roman legions encamped during the siege of Jerusalem in A.D. 70, and near here also Saladin had his headquarters when he forced the Crusaders to surrender Jerusalem to him in 1187.

From the early days of the Christian era it was the ambition of kings and warriors of European countries to have their bodies laid to rest in the sacred soil near the Holy City. The request of King Robert the Bruce to Lord Douglas to carry the heart of Bruce for burial near the Holy Sepulchre was not fulfilled, as Douglas died in the attempt. In the churchyard of a small chapel on the slope of the Mount of Olives overlooking Jerusalem there has been interred the heart of a Scottish nobleman in modern times, as is stated in a Latin inscription on a marble slab in the porch of the church. The bodies of the men of the British Expeditionary Force, from Great Britain, S. Africa, India, Australia, and New Zealand—the modern Crusaders who gave their lives in helping to free the Holy Land from the rule of the Turks—are laid to rest in a spot which overlooks the Holy City and all its hallowed surroundings.

In earth, once trodden by the Master's feet,
They lie, their bodies now at rest.
They came from far,—the sea-girt isles,
The crowded mart, the hills wind-swept,
But now they sleep in hallowed ground
O'erlooking where, of yore, the Master slept.

Their bodies, worn by toils of war,—
The midnight march, the dawn's swift, fierce attack,
Or scorched by desert's sun, or chilled by rain,
By fiery bullet scarred, or naked sword,—
Repose in dust, their souls, set free,
Are called to higher service by their Lord.

INDEX

241

INDEX

COULLS SOMERVILLE WILKIE LTD.